# Making Time

Barbara Bell

Published by Barbara Bell, 2024.

While every precaution has been taken in the preparation of this book, the publisher assumes no responsibility for errors or omissions, or for damages resulting from the use of the information contained herein.

MAKING TIME

# Table of Contents

To Esther, who makes time for making time

# Introduction:
# The Virtual Flash Mob
# of Creative Souls

You can't use up creativity.
The more you use, the more you have.
*- Maya Angelou -*

M y three brothers are all multi-talented, and one of the things they all enjoy is photography. A few years ago, when my youngest daughter was visiting her grandparents (my brother Paul and his wife live next door), Paul was showing her some of his photographs. As he discussed the kind of camera he had used, what time of day it was, the subject he had chosen, my daughter commented that he sounded just like her mom. Paul was immediately interested.

"Your mom does photography, too?"

"No," said my daughter, "but you should hear her talk about wool! She can tell you what kind of sheep it is from, where the sheep lived, what makes its wool different from some other sheep's wool..."

Spinning wool into yarn and knitting it afterward are only two of the things I get carried away talking about...maybe a bit too much. My problem is that, like my brothers, I have many things I feel that way about, but how can anyone limit herself to only one creative "passion" when the world is full of such interesting things to see and do?

Drawing might have been my first avid interest. As soon as I could hold a crayon without eating it (perhaps sooner), I was drawing pictures. Books caught up with drawing once I had gotten good at reading. Sewing, reading, writing; singing, playing musical instruments; spinning yarn, knitting, beading, embroidery; making dolls, making bread, making pottery - they've all been No. 1 in my life at one time or another, and I can talk endlessly about any of them. If you know something about these topics and can add to the conversation when we're together, great! If I can get you interested in trying one of my favorite crafts, that's even better!

In recent years I have realized that when it comes to being involved in creative activities, it's all right not to do *everything*. For example, I gave away almost all my collection of seed beads when I realized I wasn't doing much beading anymore; I saved a few packages in case I happened to need some for a project now and then. But I'll never forget learning how to apply beads, like embroidery, to leather or thick woolen cloth, when I had the privilege of taking lessons from members of the Métis Nation, the "Flower Bead People," in Canada. Métis beadwork, which draws on both First Nations and French Canadian traditions, features floral rather than geometric designs. Even though I don't do much Métis beadwork anymore, I still have the tools (and a few beads) and I know I can if I need to. When I started making tiny felt dolls a couple of years ago, I found the urge to do beadwork designs on their dresses irresistible. Everything about these dolls being so small, it didn't take long to complete a project, and the beads I had saved were more than enough for what I wanted to make.

Spinning yarn is probably among the most meditative of the crafts I have ever tried my hand at. Once you get past the first day or two of feeling like a one-man band - keeping the yarn twisting and feeding onto the bobbin evenly and the wheel turning in the same direction at the same time - the process settles into a smooth, repetitive series of small actions that's somehow extremely soothing. There was a time when I would come home from work, sit down and begin spinning. "Unwind" may sound like a joke in this context, but in my opinion there's no better way to do it than with this humble fiber craft.

Close to spinning in meditative qualities is knitting, and there are a lot more people who relax with knitting these days than there are spinners. Knitting is also more portable than most spinning. You can carry it around in a bag, get it out to work on and put it away in a moment. And with both spinning and knitting, as with many of the other crafts, after you've had your entertainment, you end up with a useful item that you can keep, give away, or even sell.

All the other skills I have picked up have had their time and place, but the one that surprised me most was probably pottery. In our town, the Senior Center offers reasonably-priced pottery classes, a fully-equipped studio and the use of a kiln along with one's yearly membership (and you qualify as a senior there at age 50.) I had never been seriously interested in pottery before because of the expense involved in setting up a kiln and all the rest of it. When those things were provided, however, I found I couldn't keep away from clay. I made one thing after another. Glazes in different colors opened another fascinating area of experimentation. My friends in the clay room would say, "When you open the kiln, it's Christmas," because you never knew exactly how things would turn out.

Speaking of Christmas, the first year I was working in clay I informed my family that, like it or not, they were all getting pottery as Christmas gifts. That was, unfortunately, the year the last load in the kiln before the holidays misfired and many of our pieces were ruined, teaching me that if you want to make Christmas gifts, it's best to start months ahead of time so you have time for do-overs if necessary. Perhaps my family was relieved not to have my beginners'-level pottery in their gift packages, after all, although (being kind people) they said nothing about it and thanked me graciously for the pieces I made for them the following Christmas. They are so gracious, my family.

I guess what I really like most - what I get most enthusiastic about - is being around other people who feel passionate about what they do. Creative people, like my brother (all my brothers, in fact), can draw you into feeling interested in their work even if you don't personally know much about it to start with. I've sat spellbound hearing a craftswoman who grows and processes her own flax give a talk about the steps that go into producing linen. Wood intrigues me; aside from the beauty of the wood and what people make from it, my brothers all work with wood. They do woodcarvings and make things like musical instruments, furniture, snowshoes and jewelry. In a local professional crafters' organization, I've come to know wood turners as well, who work with lathes. (Someday I'll try that too.)

Creativity doesn't have to only mean making things with your hands. I have enjoyed hearing a geologist talk about rocks, a history scholar recall events of the past. My brother Tim tells the best stories about the volunteer fire department he was chief of in their small town for many years. Creativity includes discoveries, inventions and scientific breakthroughs. It includes performances that lift and inspire us, whether they are by world-class artists or by our friends and family on the front porch, as neighborhood musicians have done for centuries. With the Internet, we can now find ways to enjoy these things from places we might never be able to visit in real life.

Even in movies, my favorite scene is likely to be the one where somebody is creating something. Kids' movies are good at this. The scene in Pixar's *Toy Story 2* where the repairman is fixing Woody, the vintage cowboy doll, is an example. So is the scene in *Ratatouille* where Remy, the chef who is also a rat, is correcting the seasoning of the soup that the well-meaning "garbage boy"/aspiring chef Linguini has just ruined. For grownups, *Julie & Julia* has a lot of cooking scenes – some inspirational, some near-tragic, some funny. And as I said before, it doesn't have to be someone literally creating objects with their hands. I also love those big dance sequences you often get in musicals. You know what I'm talking about: where a main character, walking down the street, begins dancing and singing his heart out - and everyone he passes suddenly knows the steps and the words and can harmonize or even chime in with counterpoint? How about *The Music Man? Or Oliver!?* Or the movie *Bride and Prejudice*, a modern retelling of the Jane Austen classic complete with exuberant song and dance scenes, centering around the lives of a family in India with several daughters of marriageable age? To those who argue, "Yeah, but people don't just break out into a choreographed song and dance number in the street like that with no warning," I would like to say that this too appears to have changed. Nowadays, you just never know. (I only wish we had more flash mobs in *my* town.)

In my ideal future world, everyone would get a chance to experiment with their creative side starting as soon as they could (for example) hold a crayon without eating it, handle tools to make useful or beautiful things, learn the steps of a dance to be shared with the community where they live, or relate stories that people will remember, be inspired by, and apply to problems in their own lives. It will take everyone who is just a little bit more advanced than these newcomers to encourage them, inviting them to use their brains, eyes, hands and feet to make the world a better, more enjoyable and more interesting place to live. Eventually, everyone would discover what his gift is, and pursue it. Wouldn't it be wonderful if when we walked out into our neighborhoods, we were met by a virtual "flash mob" of creative souls ready to tackle the problems of the world?

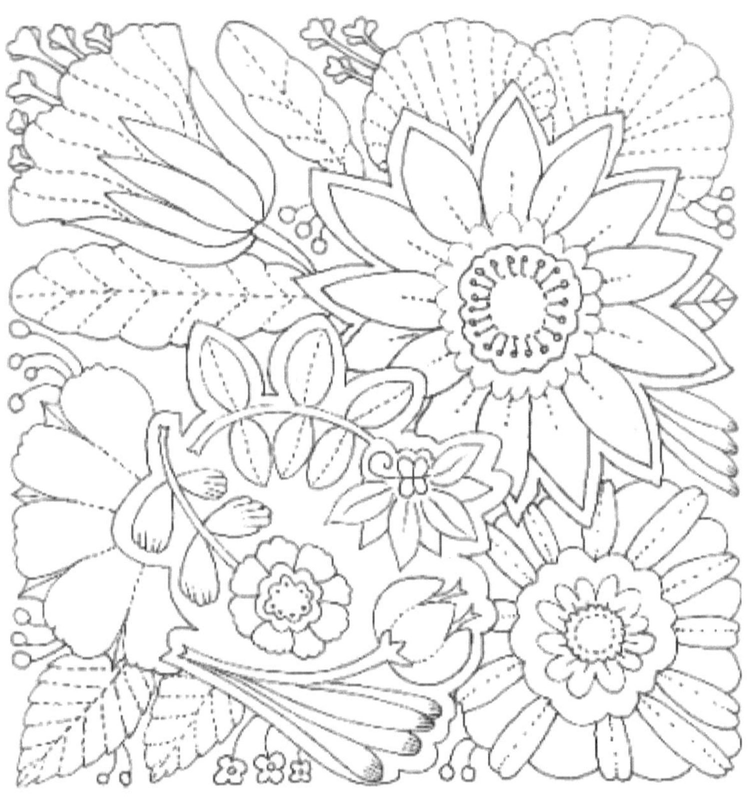

# The Restorative Art of Knitting

Sleep, that knits up the ravell'd sleave of care.
- *Shakespeare* -

———————◦———————

It all started as an experiment. Well, actually, before that it started with an emergency visit to my dentist after I woke up one day with throbbing pain and a noticeably swollen jaw. The dentist looked in my mouth and told me I had an impacted wisdom tooth and would need it pulled.

"I could do it," he explained, "but I'm going to refer you to a dental surgeon. If I did it, it would take me a lot longer and wouldn't be much fun for you. The surgeon is a specialist, very experienced; he can get it out in just a few minutes." He prescribed an antibiotic to get the infection and the swelling down, and his receptionist scheduled the surgery for a few days later

As promised, the specialist was efficient and very quick. The job was done in minutes, with no more than the usual degree of discomfort associated with any extraction under local anesthetic. Prescription in hand for heavy-duty pain medication, I decided I was feeling good enough to stop at our little neighborhood pharmacy on the way home and get it filled; there was a queue ahead of me several customers deep when I got there, but the wait probably wouldn't take long. I joined the line and waited.

It took longer than I thought it would. The local anesthetic began to wear off as I stood there. Fidgeting, I wondered why I had thought picking up anything at all on the way home from my own dental surgery would be a good idea. I could have been snugly tucked in at home with my aching jaw by now...my hero husband would be glad to drive back and get the order filled for me.

My turn came at last. I handed over the prescription, then crept back to a seat on a bench by the door next to another customer, a little white-haired lady, and waited for the pharmacist to fill it.

Five more minutes passed. Ten minutes. This wasn't much fun at all. I closed my eyes and wondered if I should just leave, drive the last few blocks home, take some over-the-counter extra-strength Tylenol, and climb into bed. The prescription meds could wait. I didn't even have a book with me to distract myself from the battle that was raging where that impacted tooth used to be. All I had was...my knitting, which I had shoved into my bag before leaving the house.

The project currently on the needles was a sock. And not just an ordinary sock either. For me - usually a plain-vanilla kind of knitter when it came to socks - this was an unusually complicated design with a 22-row pattern repeat (I would be most of the way through the first sock before I figured out the math that would help me memorize the sequence) featuring twisted stitches forming columns of scallops that looked like fish scales. In fact, the sock design, "Pomatomus," was named after a kind of fish, as I'd learned when I looked it up. I had found the pattern on Ravelry.[1] The yarn I was using was exceptionally soft - fine wool and alpaca fiber reinforced with nylon, in a deep ruby red, one of my favorite colors.

Well, at this point anything was worth a try. I dug the half-finished sock out of my bag. At worst, I'd be shoving it back into the bag a few minutes later when I found the pain wouldn't let me concentrate.

I managed to knit my way to the end of the first round. Then the second round. Was it my imagination, or was the pain beginning to recede? When the pharmacist finally called my name, I was still knitting away, the pain level had gone down to something closer to bearable, and I was ready to pay for my prescription, collect my little packet and skip out the door. Piece of cake.

It's one of those things you hear people say, but never quite know whether to believe: knitting can help with pain management. The day it actually worked for me fixed the theory in my memory in the way only personal experience can do. Unfortunately (or perhaps I should say "fortunately") I so seldom have severe pain that there hasn't been much of a chance to try it again for myself. I have, however, spoken with other knitters, some of whom suffer from debilitating medical conditions involving chronic pain. While there's a "your mileage may vary" aspect here, this kind of activity does in at least some cases seem to have benefits beyond just the eventual production of socks, mittens, sweaters and afghans.

Knitting can be comforting, soothing to body and soul. Like sleep, it can have restorative properties. It can contribute to a calm and meditative state of mind. While research shows that engaging in most handcrafts can help to maintain or regain calm in times of stress, knitting is said to be especially good for this because both hands and many parts of the brain are used, according to an article in *US News and World Report* on the health benefits of this well-known art/craft.[2] Even the position of the arms during knitting, says well-being coach Betsan Corkhill in the article, may create what feels like a "safe zone" in front of the body, giving comfort to those with anxiety issues.

Knitting is accessible. It's been around for a thousand years or so, but while on the one hand it has during its history had its guilds, its master knitters with their jealously-guarded secrets, and its mystique in the eyes of non-practitioners, it has on the other hand often been viewed as labor suitable for children and relatively unskilled adults. The tools - two or more smooth, sharpened sticks - could often be fabricated locally. Once the aspiring knitter had had a few basic lessons, he (in England, where the first English knitting guilds were male-only) or she (the women weren't far behind) would soon be producing knitwear for the family or for sale.

Another aspect of knitting that many find comforting is its well-known social side. Who hasn't heard of the "knitting circles" of the past cranking out warm fuzzies for new babies, the poor, the sick, members of the military, or disaster victims? Such voluntary associations of knitters donating to charity still exist (you can ask at your local yarn shop, if you're looking for one near you; churches are another possibility.) Whether they are loving friends and family members or compassionate strangers, many knitters have learned that this craft - essentially a one-person job - can be even more enjoyable when practiced for a good cause, and in the company of other knitters.

There's even some evidence that a troubled person may be more inclined to open up and talk when his or her conversation partner is knitting. Maybe the deep sense of calm that flows over many a knitter-at-work is contagious. Maybe it's the "I'm all ears, but I don't need to stare at you every minute while you unburden your soul - go ahead and talk" attitude of such knitters that helps in this regard. Although situations vary, in many cases being in the presence of a knitter does seem to ease tension and may help open a path of communication.

Any experienced knitter will tell you that knitting can be an expensive habit, but that it doesn't have to be. The *feel* of the yarn is important, and while truly luxurious yarns (cashmere!) tend to be pricey, there are yarns that are almost as soft as cashmere and much more affordable. Knitters will "pet" the yarn when making a selection - stroking it, carrying it around for a few minutes, perhaps holding it against the more sensitive inner wrist/elbow or the side of the face (taking care to avoid sharing germs - and makeup) to see how soft it is. Part of what makes knitting such a soothing activity is the way it feels.

Speaking of soothing, how many times do we stress out over things we think we should do, but don't have time for? Just tracking down appropriate gifts for people we like, as much fun as it is supposed to be, can be that kind of stressor. What if, during otherwise unoccupied moments, you knew you could work on something easy, comforting, and relatively mindless that would end up as a gift? What if you knew that weeks and months of these easy and comforting sessions of practicing a relatively uncomplicated craft could produce a stack of gifts, all ready for the next holiday, wedding, student graduation or birth of a child? These gifts don't need to be six-foot-long scarves, multi-textured fisherman sweaters or afghans the size of a double bed; although all these things certainly have their good points, there are hundreds of patterns for small, thoughtful gift items many people would be delighted to receive.

One of my personal favorites is an Illusion knit dishcloth, for which free patterns are available online. This intriguing technique, also called "shadow knitting," produces an item bearing text or an image *visible only from a certain angle*. If you have cotton yarn in two contrasting colors, and can knit, purl, and count up to about 42, you can make one of these. Let's face it: everyone who maintains a home with a kitchen needs something to wipe down the counters with. Why shouldn't it be something interesting? Something that, while masquerading as a common kitchen cleaning item, may when properly viewed reveal a mysterious hidden message? (For the more ambitious, there are larger Illusion knit projects - scarves, shawls, even wall hangings featuring the Mona Lisa, Marilyn Monroe or Elvis.)

This is what I call a multi-purpose hobby: for the sake of my mental health, I engage in an activity that will eventually solve numerous stressful gift-giving dilemmas, thus maintaining my own inner tranquility while at the same time doing what I can to make the outer world a better place, one dishcloth at a time.

Reading, writing, meditative drawing; walking, running, gardening; other fiber and textile arts - they all have their place in the quest to restore life's balance and alleviate stress, but I would like to suggest that knitting is one of the basics. It's not hard to learn, requires no special talent, involves simple hand-held tools, need not be expensive, is beneficial to mind and body, can be engaged in with other people around, can be engaged in *for* other people while offering numerous advantages for the knitter, and - depending on the project - may be small enough to carry around on one's person, like the fancy sock I dug out of my bag that day at the pharmacy when I discovered how good knitting could be at managing pain. In short, it is a good way to take a break from daily life stress even when you can't actually step aside from daily life.

Shakespeare may or may not have been a knitter, but based on the metaphor he employed comparing it to sleep, I think he knew what he was talking about.

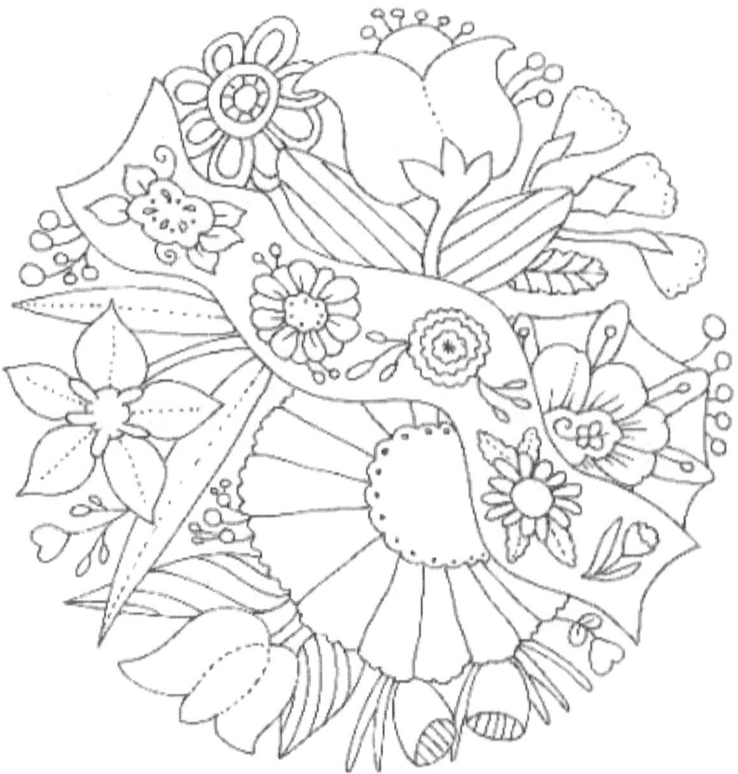

# Office-Based Home

Let me but do my work from day to day,
In field or forest, at the desk or loom,
In roaring market-place or tranquil room;
Let me but find it in my heart to say,
When vagrant wishes beckon me astray,
"This is my work; my blessing, not my doom;
"Of all who live, I am the one by whom
"This work can best be done in the right way."
Then shall I see it not too great, nor small,
To suit my spirit and to prove my powers;
Then shall I cheerful greet the labouring hours,
And cheerful turn, when the long shadows fall
At eventide, to play and love and rest,
Because I know for me my work is best.
- *Henry van Dyke* -

It was only after getting his master's degree in music theory that my dad figured he had made a mistake: he should have gone for music education instead, which would have made it easier to find a job. So, for the next few years, he tried his hand at different things, some of which included music (he was conducting a high-school band the year I was born) and many of which didn't. He worked for a while in a photography studio, then a florist's shop. He even sold insurance for a couple of years.

One day he and Mom saw an advertisement in a music magazine: "Learn to do music engraving at home!" The ad showed a picture of a special typewriter that typed music notes and symbols instead of letters and numbers. With this machine, you could create "camera-ready" documents that could then be used as master copies for publishing sheet music and books.

In the 1960s, this was cutting-edge technology, a modern improvement over previous music typewriters, and much advanced from the way music had formerly been printed from hand-engraved lead or copper plates (even now, with the work being done digitally, the procedure is still referred to as "engraving.") My parents discussed the matter and decided to order one of these typewriters, thinking that Mom - who did have a master's degree in music ed but was now busy at home raising us four kids - might be able to do music transcription in her spare time.

When the typewriter arrived, however, Dad, who had been transcribing music by hand as a hobby since his school days, found he couldn't stay away from it. He spent hours playing with it, finding out what it would do. Eventually, he taught himself the necessary skills, set up a home office, and literally hung out his shingle - a black-and-white sign he designed and painted himself - from a pole in our front yard: **Music Manuscript Service.**

Dad has now been a home-based freelance music engraver for around 60 years. To be precise, he's been retired for about half that time, but he continues to do it just for fun - which is the kind of job I'd like to have when I retire.

He used to set up his office anywhere it would fit, in whatever house we were living in at the time. It might be in the dining room, a spare bedroom, an enclosed front porch, the basement.

All the desks in Dad's office were made of wooden doors with detachable hardware-store legs. Every desk had a drawing board, propped up to the correct angle with stacks of books. The rest of every surface would be covered with tools and materials - reams of paper, technical pens and blue pencils, bottles of India ink and correction fluid; rubber cement and other kinds of glue; various rulers and templates; and miscellaneous devices such as a bendable curved-edge tool that *would* have been fun for my brothers and me to play with, if we'd been allowed.

The central item in the office was the music typewriter, but there were also two sleek, modern alphanumeric typewriters, each with a different font, for adding text to the music. All three of these typewriters had special one-use-only carbon tape that produced very clear, sharp impressions. There was a fourth typewriter, too - one Dad didn't use in his work. It was there for an important reason.

Both our parents liked for us kids to stay busy. Expensive toys were out of the question, since Dad's work just about paid for the basics - food, housing, car, clothes - but not much more than that. If we asked them to buy us something that other kids were getting, they (like other frugal-minded parents of that era) usually said they couldn't afford it; we were too poor. However, when it came to activities that were educational, or that involved making or building something...well, that category *was* basic. There were limits, of course, but within the budget, if you were being creative - if you were learning or practicing a useful skill, whether it was sewing, carpentry, art or music - a way could often be found to get the supplies you needed.

Mom used to do craft projects with us at the dining-room table, getting us in the habit, as she would say later, of being too busy to get into trouble (it didn't always work, but think of the trouble we would have gotten into without it.) There was, of course, lots of music. We all had at least a few piano lessons from Mom; we all learned harmony by singing rounds together at dinnertime and in the car, sometimes the traditional ones such as "Row, Row, Row Your Boat," but often rounds that Dad wrote for us. And when we were old enough, we would sometimes be allowed to spend time with Dad in his office.

That was what the fourth typewriter was for. An old-fashioned model, high and black and rickety-looking, bashing out letters in a Courier-style font with a reusable cloth ribbon that produced legible, if fuzzy-looking, print, it was for us kids to type on whenever we visited the office, since Dad was not about to let us pound on his good equipment for our own entertainment. We wouldn't be allowed to use the special, professional typewriters until we had learned to type properly, in school, and could prove it.

Dad enjoyed listening to music while he worked - most of the time, in fact - so his record player, large collection of LP vinyl records, and eventually a big reel-to-reel tape recorder and stacks of flat boxes containing tapes took up most of one wall. In later years he wired our entire house for sound so we could all wake up to music in the morning (the speakers in each room could be disconnected when we wanted it quiet.) What he played might be classical, modern, or his favorite Spike Jones, forerunner and inspiration to comedy musicians of later generations such as "Weird Al" Yankovic. Early exposure to Spike Jones is doubtless to blame for my lifelong inability to take seriously the sentimental or angst-ridden popular music of any generation. I mean, how can a person keep a straight face when she can't help imagining the crashes, bangs, whistles, screams of laughter, well-timed commentary, revving motorcycle engines, and other sound effects that so many contemporary "Top 10" musicians have mysteriously left out of their work? And if it weren't for *artistes* like Spike Jones and "Weird Al," how would we ever learn that we need a healthy balance between sentiment and humor?

One day I noticed a tiny, typewritten paper tag Scotch-taped to one of the wires connecting the complex homemade "sound system" spread across the wall of Dad's office, which was in our dining room at that time. Curious, I leaned closer and closer until I was able to make out the little note. It said,

*wire you reading this?*

Anything displayed on the walls of Dad's office was going to be of some significance, humorous or otherwise. Along with jokes like the "wire" tag were other messages that were more thought-provoking, such as a line attributed to violin maker Antonio Stradivarius. Years later, when I looked up this quote online, I found it in a poem by George Eliot:

*If I slack my hand, I rob God,*
*for God cannot make a Stradivarius violin.*

And this one, which I still see on the wall behind my dad when we video-chat every week:

THIMK

Like most kids, I was drawing pictures long before I could read, but by the time I was in school it was my free-time activity of choice. Mom, who had started all us kids off early doing crafts to get us in the habit of making things, believed along with Dad that you would know what a person's talents were by what they would work at when nobody was making them do it. When you had figured this out, then you could nurture it in them.

As soon as Dad thought I could be trusted with India ink (perhaps by the time I was seven or eight) he put aside one of his older technical pens for me. He showed me how to clean and fill it, and when I went into the office to visit him, he'd set me up at a drawing board with a stack of good-one-side manuscript scrap paper. Thus equipped, I could draw and listen to music for hours.

Dad, busy at his own work, would comment occasionally on what was playing:

"If you listen, you'll hear the 'Frère Jacques' theme in this movement, but in a minor key." (Mahler's "Symphony No. 1")

"Did you catch 'Pop Goes the Weasel' there?" ("The Moldau," by Smetana)

One afternoon, he put a recording on, then suggested I draw whatever the music sounded like to me. He often saved my pictures and tacked them up around the office, and he was really cross with me the day he found out I had taken one of these pictures off the wall to give to a friend of mine who was visiting. "That was one of my favorites!" he protested.

Since Dad was the only coffee-drinker in the family, the coffee pot lived in his office along with the other tools of his trade. Dad would sometimes offer me a taste even when I was too young to indulge. He'd say, "Go get your cup," I'd bring one of my doll's teacups, he'd pour me about a tablespoonful, and we'd have our coffee break together. He preferred it strong and black, and when as an adult I did start drinking coffee regularly, I decided I liked it better with cream, eventually abandoning "real" coffee for decaf most of the time. But strong, black coffee, whenever I have occasion to drink it that way, still reminds me of my dad's office - my little doll's teacup, a half-finished drawing on the board, music in the background.

After he retired, Dad found he couldn't keep away from music engraving, the same as with the music typewriter back in the early days. So he just kept going, preparing sheet music for songwriters among friends and acquaintances who might never have seen their original compositions in print before. He'll offer to do it for complete strangers, like my friends, who sometimes take him up on it.

In the early 1990s he found out about a computer program for engraving music. Dad promptly ordered the program, and a computer to install it on. It took him about six weeks to teach himself how to use the program. After that, he never looked back. Now, when I walk into his office, his computer, printer and electronic piano keyboard occupy the space where the music typewriter and drawing boards once stood. He still plays music recordings, but the vinyl record collection and reel-to-reel tapes have been replaced by Internet music channels and YouTube videos.

People often consider their mother's kitchen to have been the heart of their childhood home. In my case, the kitchen and dining room - where we had our meals, then did our homework, read aloud and sang together - shared "heart of the home" status with my dad's office. Mom helped him with his work when he was up against a deadline; he in turn helped in the kitchen (homemade bread and pizza!) or picked one of us up from an after-school event when needed. I didn't realize till after I was grown up myself how unusual this arrangement was, back in the days before the term "working from home" had come into common usage, and even now it's a privilege not every family is in a position to enjoy. I could wish it for everyone, though.

Maybe Dad's getting his degree in music theory instead of music education back at the university hadn't been such a bad idea after all.

# Creating Calm,
# One Detail at a Time

Photography is an immediate reaction,
drawing is a meditation.
*- Henri Cartier-Bresson -*

There was, I think, a gap of about ten years between when my parents thought I was old enough to sit quietly through a church service, and when *I* thought I was. It's not that I wasn't listening to the preacher or didn't remember anything he said during those years. Certainly I paid close attention whenever he told any stories. And I enjoyed singing all the hymns, which might have been my favorite part of any church service. Like most kids, I chose hearty participation over passive inaction in any long grown-up meeting, so a long hymn with five verses was much better than a short one with only two. Now and then, whoever planned the service would decide we needed to sing only the first and last verses of some hymn. I would glance longingly at the unused verses as we sang past them, thinking of all the good music we were missing. When I was old enough, I joined the choir and sang with the other choir members up front behind the waist-high paneled wall that separated the choir from the preacher. But when we settled back to listen to the sermon, I usually drew pictures on the margins of the church bulletin.

Some of us seem to be able to listen better when we are doing something with our hands. I had begun drawing as soon as I could hold a crayon without eating it (possibly sooner) and drawing quickly became one of my favorite activities. At home, our parents saved good-one-side junk mail and office scrap paper in a box for my brothers and me to draw on. We did so much drawing that sometimes we actually ran out of paper. It was disconcerting to go to the box for another piece and find it empty, and Mom eventually began buying the ends of rolls of blank newsprint from the newspaper office, thus augmenting the erratic supply of good-one-side scrap paper. You could draw *really* big pictures with a sheet of newsprint cut from a roll.

Complex doodles covered every blank paper I had on me when I was away from home, such as the bulletins that kept me, a restless child, quiet in church. Disposable paper tablecloths at a banquet, for example, were wonderful. You could draw on these while speakers droned on and on; the tablecloths were just going to be thrown away anyhow. If you were really strapped for drawing material, paper napkins worked as long as you had a ball-point pen, although with pencils they weren't quite as satisfactory.

When you do enough doodling, sooner or later a picture worth saving is going to appear, but some of my best ones were ending up in the trash after a banquet, or crumpled and smudged at the bottom of my purse. I would be well along in middle age before it occurred to me that this was a problem I could do something about. I began carrying a small sketchbook and drawing pens among my personal accoutrements, along with my driver's license, debit card, cell phone and water bottle. Thus, "doodling," a lifelong habit begun in childhood to stave off boredom, would eventually shift toward what has been called "meditative drawing."

Most of my life I have preferred representational drawing. My favorite subject - people - eventually led to my taking lessons in portraiture. I told myself I wasn't particularly interested in anything abstract or symbolic. I didn't expect anyone to peer at one of my portraits and say to himself, "I sense a great deal of anger in this picture," or "She must have been going through a period when she felt blue," or "In this painting we hear the soul of the artist crying out against the heartless materialism of modern society." No, you would look at one of my pictures and say, "Hmm, that's a girl with curly pigtails, in a pink jacket," or "This man is wearing a baseball cap that says, 'Birthplace of Country Music Alliance,' and holding a guitar," or "That teenaged boy doing his homework at the kitchen table has a cat on his lap." You could form your own conclusions about what each piece meant, and have your own emotional reactions, but there was no doubt about what I was actually representing.

Meditative drawing was different. In general, it wasn't representational. It was unlike other activities I enjoyed such as sewing or knitting; it didn't produce anything useful, wasn't always beautiful, and might not have furthered any skill except that of being able to do it better, yet at some undefined time in the recent past - I don't remember exactly when - it became one of the chief art forms that I, a lifelong representational artist, found myself practicing.

I was still making serious art, usually portraits - the kind you could get commissions for. With meditative drawings, it was fun to create designs that didn't have to amount to anything. I could refine my technique to be more symmetrical or varied, but only if I wanted to. If I didn't like what I had drawn, it was easy to turn the page and start a new drawing. If I liked something I had drawn, I could use the same shapes and lines over and over again in subsequent drawings.

In many art styles, one conceives of the whole, plans a composition and then fills in the details. In meditative drawing, also sometimes called "expandism," one starts with a single detail and *expands,* or builds outward from it. When I create a meditative drawing, I seldom plan it out ahead of time. Usually I just start drawing, and add details as they occur to me.

A meditative drawing can be symmetrical but need not be. It can start in the middle, but it might also develop off to one side, grow from the top or the bottom, or blossom from one of the corners of the paper. It may end up being startlingly beautiful or it might be nothing special to look at, but because such a drawing is typically quite small (mine are about 4" x 4"; Zentangle® artists go even smaller, about 3" x 3") it won't be long before you finish one and can start over again on a fresh piece of paper.

Although the point of a meditative drawing is to enjoy the process itself rather than to create a realistic picture, mine sometimes do have representations included in them. Flowers and leaves, a book, a cup, a piece of fruit, a bird, a fish, furniture, windows, roads...I have used all these in my meditative drawings at times. I just don't try to compose a realistic picture based on any of them.

I make templates from card stock and keep one or two tucked into a half envelope glued inside the front of my sketchbook. My familiarity with junk mail as artists' material has influenced my decision to save advertising cards with pretty pictures on them and cut them into 4" x 4" squares for templates. Why should I use a new piece of blank card stock that I probably paid good money for, when I could have a square of thick, glossy card stock printed in many bright colors that arrived free of charge in the mail - a gift from someone who wants to do business with me - bearing a real estate agent's picture of a house for sale, or a group of laughing college students? This is also a good way to make use of some of those beautiful Christmas cards I get every year. When a template gets too worn, I can throw it out and make a new one.

After tracing a square on a blank page with one of my templates, I begin filling the square with lines and shapes. I work without hurrying. Especially where two lines meet or two shapes touch, it pays to slow way, *way* down and use care. This is not a race. This is a meditative practice. I can think about things while I am drawing, and I do. That's why it is called "meditative."

I can add text to my drawing, too. In fact, sometimes I start one of my drawings with a name, a word, a phrase or more, and develop the picture around the text. It's a fun way to take notes when I am in a class or a meeting and want to remember what is being said. Later, I will have to hunt through my sketchbooks to find these notes, so using meditative drawing as a note-taking technique works best for very short meetings where everything I might want to remember can be packed into a 4" x 4" square along with any doodles I've added during the meeting.

While my meditative drawings are something I create just for myself and for the fun of it, I often give them away (or even, occasionally, sell one). One year I gift-wrapped one of my filled sketchbooks as a Christmas present for a friend who had told me she loved my drawings. The next year, she gave me a portfolio with a sketchpad and elastic pockets for colored pencils in it. Suddenly, my meditative drawing went off in a new direction. I had never thought of coloring my little drawings, but why shouldn't I? Thus, I joined the ranks of those who have adopted "adult coloring" as a meditative activity.

I've filmed myself creating these drawings, and I've shared the videos on YouTube and the completed pictures on Facebook and elsewhere for others to print and color. One reason I have filmed the process is because while a finished meditative drawing can appear surprisingly complex, it is based on very simple shapes and lines. I wanted to show such a drawing from beginning to end, thinking viewers might be encouraged to try it themselves if they saw it broken down into steps.

It's art anyone can create - anyone who can print letters and numbers, draw a simple shape or a line, or hold a crayon, pen, pencil or marker without eating it. And if you don't like your first one, turn the page and start over again. This art form is about the process, not the results. Of course, if you do like your first one and the ones that come after it, you can turn the page and start over again too. There's nothing like lots of practice. And if you find yourself drawing a lot, I urge you to invest in a sketchbook. You never know where it might end up, and it's wise to treat your art with the respect it deserves.

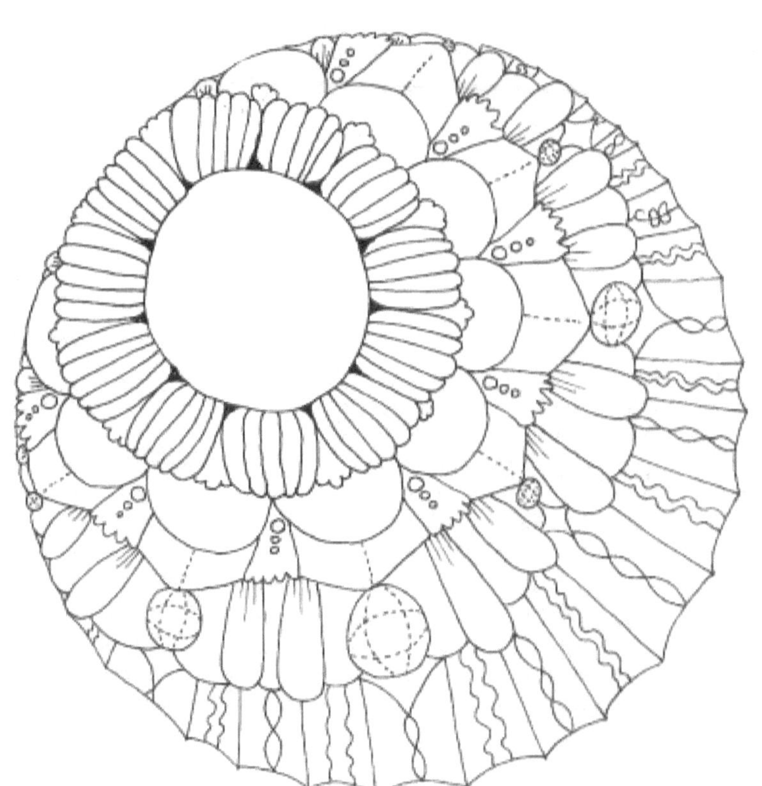

# A Stitch in Timelessness

Take your needle, my child, and work at your pattern;
it will come out a rose by and by. Life is like that –
one stitch at a time taken patiently and the pattern
will come out all right like the embroidery.
*- Oliver Wendell Holmes -*

The most ambitious hand-sewing project I ever undertook was a plaid flannel shirt for my fiancé. I was twenty-one, I'd been using a sewing machine since I was eight, and I hadn't intended to sew this shirt by hand - I knew from having three brothers that guys could be hard on their clothes, and I assumed the shirt would need machine-sewn seams and buttonholes if it was to stand up to the rough wear I expected my intended to give it (he was working in a sawmill at the time.)

But then something came up. I was going to be spending a few weeks that fall with friends "off the grid." We would be traveling by canoe and on foot, so I was trying to think of some kind of handcraft project I could bring with me that wouldn't take up too much room in my backpack. There was no electricity where I was going; even if there had been, I wasn't about to lug my sewing machine out there. My mom suggested I cut the shirt out and take the pieces with me to sew by hand.

"Mom, that would take forever."

"You might be surprised how quickly it would go together," she said.

Not fully convinced, but wanting my fiancé to get a plaid flannel shirt made by me while the weather was still cold enough for him to wear it, and not having any reasonable alternatives for handcraft projects to be completed while staying in a log cabin in the woods with no electricity (I hadn't yet fully engaged with knitting, as I would later on), I stuffed the unfinished shirt and my sewing supplies into the backpack, under my other belongings.

Not long after we arrived at our remote northern wilderness cabin, the temperature dropped suddenly and the lake outside our front door froze over like a sheet of glass in a single, still night. We couldn't go anywhere for a few days, since there was too much ice for canoes and not enough yet for snowshoes, so along with the wood-chopping and water-carrying of our normal days, we hung around the cabin making popcorn and hot chocolate, catching up on our reading, goofing around on the ice near the shores of the lake, having snowball fights and building snowmen after we got a storm or two, and generally attempting to avoid cabin fever while in a state of enforced isolation. (Interesting fact: sticks and stones skipped across the surface of a smoothly frozen lake slide a long, long way, and make very interesting sounds. You can look this up on YouTube.)

One day while we were still waiting for the ice to get thick enough for travel, I dug out my fiancé's shirt from the bottom of my backpack and began to sew. It did go together much more quickly than I'd expected. Here I was with time on my hands and limited entertainment options - what else was I going to do? Instead of the weeks I had envisioned this project taking, it was finished in about three days, and when I got home I had a handmade shirt to give my guy...a shirt he ended up wearing for years. The fabric eventually wore out. The seams never did.

I have never since made another hand-sewn shirt, but I stored the memory away: hand-sewing doesn't take as long as you think it might, and it could be just as durable as machine-sewing. However, at home there were other responsibilities waiting for me. I went back to doing most of my sewing by machine.

We got married the spring after I made that shirt, we started our family, and I was busier than I'd ever been before. The fastest and best way to make anything - that was what I wanted when the children were little. Generally, I didn't think I had time for slow, leisurely methods if there was a fast way to do it, and the single hand-stitched baby quilt I managed to finish (it took me four or five years) only convinced me that if I had ever had any interest in completing a project without the use of a sewing machine, the time for that was in the past. Besides, nowadays I wasn't spending weeks off the grid in wilderness log cabins far from sources of electricity.

My eventual re-introduction to doing things by hand the slow way was probably not sewing, but knitting. What got me interested in knitting again after a hiatus of many years was the (then) new self-patterning yarns. They would create colorwork designs in your socks by themselves as you knitted. These yarns weren't cheap, but a relative who worked at a yarn shop gave me a Christmas present one year of a bag of assorted self-patterning sock yarns she had collected from the sales bin, and that was all I knitted with as long as it lasted.

Soon I found myself returning to hand-sewing as well, at least for some projects. I began adding hand-embroidered details to garments I had sewed on the machine, and I found it relaxing. *No, this piece is not going to be finished today. It might take a few sessions to finish, but why rush if there isn't a deadline? Even if there is one - say, Christmas - why not start a few months early and take it easy? So many of our activities require us to move fast, finish on time, increase productivity. Why not have a few things in our repertoire with which we can slow down?*

These were also the years in which I was working on my skills as a dollmaker. I had already begun experimentally using upcycled, rather than new, fabrics for my dolls, collecting used clothing in good condition so I could cut it up and make it into something else, saving even buttons and zippers whenever possible. Now, I decided to sew a pair of dolls, a boy and a girl, completely by hand from upcycled fabric. Again, I was amazed at how long it *didn't* take to complete the project.

Then it was the end of the spring semester of my first year in college. I'd been a senior citizen back in school after more than forty years away from academia; I was tired of assignments and deadlines, and ready for a break. Needing something fresh in the creative realm, I turned away for a while from my regular machine-sewing, mending and knitting and decided to try my hand at making miniature, hand-sewn dolls from felt.

The pattern I found on Etsy was called "Pocket Fairy" (the doll even had an optional set of little felt wings attached with a snap.)[3] The finished model was said to be able to fit into an Altoids box. Mine didn't, quite, but at four inches high it was one of the smallest dolls I had ever made. The merino wool felt I had ordered online for the project was soft and luxurious. I couldn't afford a whole yard of it, but a quarter of a yard was enough to make lots of Pocket Fairies.

For weeks, I hand-sewed every day. I would finish one doll and start another one immediately. Over time, I ordered more of the merino felt in different skin tones, and small amounts of combed wool and silky mohair fiber for every hair color I could imagine. A five-ounce "grab bag" of scraps of the same felt in a rainbow of colors gave me more than enough material for their tiny dresses, each one differently hand-embroidered or decorated with beads.

Working on those little felt dolls and other hand-sewing projects made me feel as if I had stepped back into a world I hadn't visited in a long, long time. I'd first learned to sew from my mother and grandmother as a young child, but whenever I had attempted to make anything very small in those early days, my lack of coordination had frustrated me. Although I became more proficient as I reached my teens, other interests and responsibilities had soon crowded out the leisure I had for such pursuits. Now, as an older adult I had the patience and skill I had so wished for when I was a child, along with the time and attention to give to it that weren't available to me as a young mother.

Hand-sewing takes time, there's no question about that. But there are advantages to the slow, old-fashioned way. For one thing, it needs less space. A tabletop is nice, but for hand-sewing a lap may be good enough. For another thing, hand-sewing is quiet. It won't disturb people's conversation, the book being read aloud or the movie being watched. A third advantage is the simplicity of the tools. I have had my sewing machine break down in the middle of a big project (with a deadline, no less) and have had to try to figure out what to do next. Buy a new one? Borrow one from a friend? (The last time this happened to me, none of my friends who lived nearby owned a sewing machine they could loan me.) With hand-sewing, as long as I have a few extra needles, good scissors and plenty of thread, I'm usually pretty well set.

But I'd have to say the time required to complete a project is in itself one of the chief advantages of hand sewing. Slow down...zoom in. Pay attention to those few stitches you are looking at, instead of worrying about how many of them it will take to finish what you're working on. We only think of it as slow because we have had over a hundred and fifty years of history with sewing machines to give us the idea that it should go faster.

Until the mid-nineteenth century, everyone in the world who sewed, in every culture, sewed everything by hand. And yes, they often got impatient and wished there was a way to make it faster, and eventually someone invented a machine that lifted off the shoulders of the world's sewists the great burden of having to sew everything by hand, thus freeing their time up for other pursuits. (Laura Ingalls Wilder, author of the classic *Little House* book series, remembered realizing as a young adult that Ma hated sewing as much as she did - and the day her father came home with a treadle sewing machine in the wagon for Ma, Laura knew that he knew it, too.) Until the advent of the sewing machine, people knew how long a hand-sewn project would take and they allowed time for it, just as when we walk to the library or the grocery store we know it will take longer than if we drive, and we allow for the difference. Sometimes we don't have the time. Sometimes we do.

While I still do most of my sewing by machine, I've welcomed hand-sewing back into my life, with its calming rhythms and its limitations. I'll finish as much today as I have time for, and I'll relax and enjoy making those little seams, one stitch at a time.

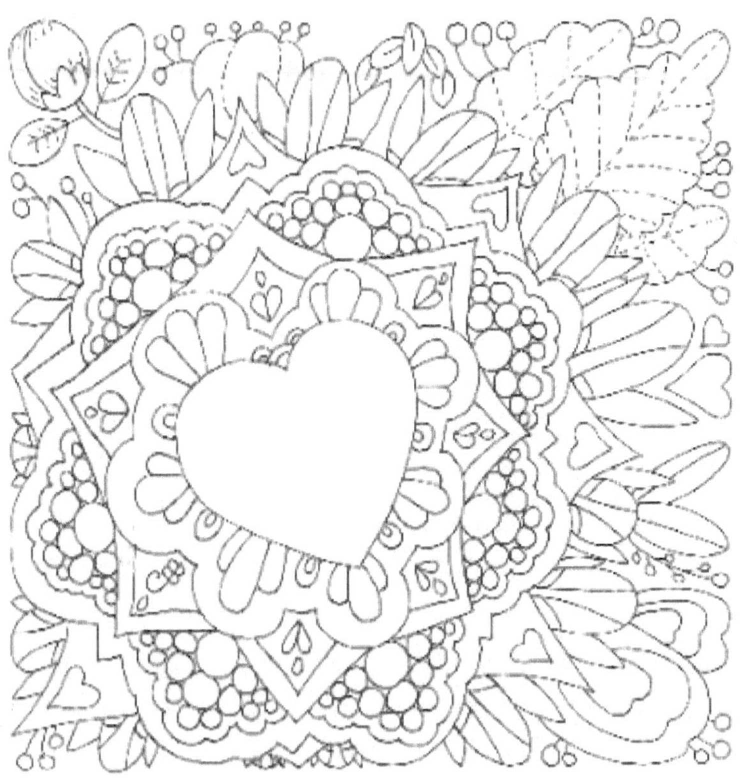

# The Battle of the Blouse

Love does not begin and end
the way we seem to think it does.
Love is a battle, love is a war;
love is a growing up.
*- James Baldwin -*

T he worst fight my mom and I ever had over clothes happened the winter I was in the fifth grade. It was the worst, but it was also one of the last.

We were poor. At least, that's what my parents always told my three brothers and me when we wanted things. Dad worked from home as a freelance music engraver, occasionally selling one of his original compositions; Mom taught piano lessons on the side. With extremely careful budgeting there was enough for our family to live on (one of my dad's regular clients, a music publishing house, paid for a year's work at a time) but most other purchases tended to be a no-go. Sure, we had food to eat and decent clothing, a car that got us from here to there, and electricity and running water in a house which, while older, had a good roof and floors - all considered luxuries in many parts of the world. What we didn't have was money for what our parents considered luxuries.

Expensive food, for example, was a luxury. I recall a dispute Mom and I had on the subject of a certain popular fast-food restaurant, whose TV commercials in those early years were already getting a lot of attention. They certainly got mine. I tried one out on Mom in the kitchen one day while she was cooking supper.

"One person can buy a whole meal there for sixty cents!" (Back then, you really could...if the "meal" was nothing more than a small hamburger, small fries and a small soft drink.)

Mom just laughed. "I can cook a meal for our whole family for sixty cents," she said.

Modestly-priced non-basic purchases were likely to come our way only at Christmas, on our birthdays, and on what my dad called "un-birthdays," a term borrowed from Lewis Carroll's *Through the Looking Glass*. In our home, Christmas and birthday gifts were often provided from the S&H Green Stamps catalog, but un-birthdays were funded by royalty payments from the sale of my dad's original compositions. If such a payment was sizable enough (I recall one arriving at our house in the form of a handful of postage stamps) my parents would use the money to buy some kind of personally significant gift for each of the children. That was how I received a beginner's set of oil paints when I was ten years old - my introduction to the world of grown-up art materials; in the distant future, I would do commissioned work as a portrait artist - and how my younger brother got a toy clarinet at the age of eight or nine, which may have inspired his learning to play a real one in the school band a few years later. But other than the infrequent royalty check, most money went to pay bills.

When it came to decent clothing, my brothers could pass many wearables down from oldest to youngest. It was a bit more complicated for me, the only girl. Mom and Grandma sewed some for me, but both were busy and didn't have time to make everything. Thrift and consignment shops were not as common, or as stylish, as they were to become later on, and ready-made clothes could be expensive.

Now, one of my mother's cousins had two daughters just slightly older than I, and their family was slightly better off financially than ours. That's where most of my school wardrobe came from. I was fine with this arrangement; it meant getting all those "new" clothes a couple of times a year, especially the ones that Mom would never have spent money on for me herself. Sweaters in real Shetland wool or mohair...party dresses with stiff crinoline underskirts...patent leather shoes in colors to match the party dresses...Mom's cousin had excellent taste as well as money, so most of the things were beautiful. Who cared that the fashions might be several years out of date by the time I got them? For a long time, *beautiful* meant more to me than *fashionable.*

By the time I was in the fifth grade, I was playing the flute in our elementary school band, and several times a year there would be a concert. In our school, as in most, a student concert was the simplest of exercises in trying to make everyone look as much as possible like everyone else. We were told to wear white shirts or blouses, with dark-colored pants for the boys and skirts for the girls. Neither fashion nor beauty should have been an issue. The dark skirt would be all right - I usually had a suitable one; but how could I forget the time Mom and I went toe-to-toe over the blouse I wanted to wear?

My favorite blouse that year was, like the rest of my school clothes, a hand-me-down, but it was beautiful: white, full-sleeved, with pintucks and silver embroidery down the front on either side of the button placket, and ruffles edged with silver stitching around the cuffs and collar. I felt like a princess in that blouse, but at an age when I was just beginning to notice fashion trends, I also thought it was similar enough to what the other girls would be wearing that I would blend in. I fully expected to wear it to the band concert. I may have even mentioned this ahead of time to Mom, in case it needed laundering.

The evening of the concert, she sent me upstairs to change into the clean clothes she had left on my bed, but when I walked into my room, instead of my favorite blouse I found a plain white cotton knit top waiting for me...a polo shirt. Brand new and spotless (Mom did catch a good sale now and then) but still, a polo shirt. The kind you might wear at summer camp with shorts and flip-flops - *not* to perform in a concert.

Appalled, I marched to the top of the stairs and, from that height, confronted my mother.

"I don't want to wear *that shirt*. I want to wear my favorite blouse. Where is it?"

Mom came to the foot of the stairs. "You can't wear that. It's not fit to be seen."

I didn't see why not. My favorite blouse was old, to be sure; the ruffles down the front and around the cuffs were ragged, the contrast stitching and embroidery missing a few - *only* a few threads, and there might even have been stains on it, not that I had paid much attention. But still, it was beautiful. The cotton knit top, on the other hand, was - well, like something you would wear to summer camp. With shorts and flip-flops.

Mom and I had a brief, heated argument. I brought eloquence and logic to my case ("None of the other girls will be wearing a *T-shirt!*"), but she stood firm. Finally, crying, I went back to my bedroom, where I pulled the boring cotton knit shirt on over my head.

I was standing there - dressed, ready to go, and feeling lonely and ugly - when I heard Mom come upstairs. Without a word, she took my hand and led me into her room where, from her closet, she pulled a silky white blouse of her own. It had elbow sleeves gathered into cuffs, and a soft tie collar. She helped me take off the plain knit shirt. Then she dressed me in her own blouse and tied the bow under my chin.

At eleven, I wasn't yet quite as big as my mom. Her blouse drooped on me, but after we tucked it into my skirt, it wasn't too noticeable. At least it wasn't a t-shirt. Even if I couldn't wear my favorite embroidered blouse, I knew I would look beautiful at the concert.

That could have been the end of this story, but it wasn't. When we walked into the auditorium later that evening, some of the band members were already on stage, chatting as they got their instruments out and arranged their music...and at least two or three of the girls, including one whose sense of style I had always secretly admired, were wearing plain white cotton knit tops similar to the one I had rejected.

I peeked sideways at my mom, who said only, "You see, it really would have been all right."

I have no idea what I would have learned from this experience if my mom hadn't come to my rescue with her own blouse. She risked triggering a complete preadolescent meltdown - an eleven-year-old could have interpreted the suggestion that she appear in public in her mother's blouse as an invitation to war. Instead, Mom's actions helped neutralize the bitterness of many future mother-daughter disagreements over clothing styles. Maybe I didn't get my way, but - to be fair - neither did she. I also got my first glimpse of the fickleness of fashion and eventually decided it wasn't worth getting all worked up over.

Mom learned something, too. The next time she checked out a sale on girls' ready-made clothes, she brought me along with her. But that's a story for another time.

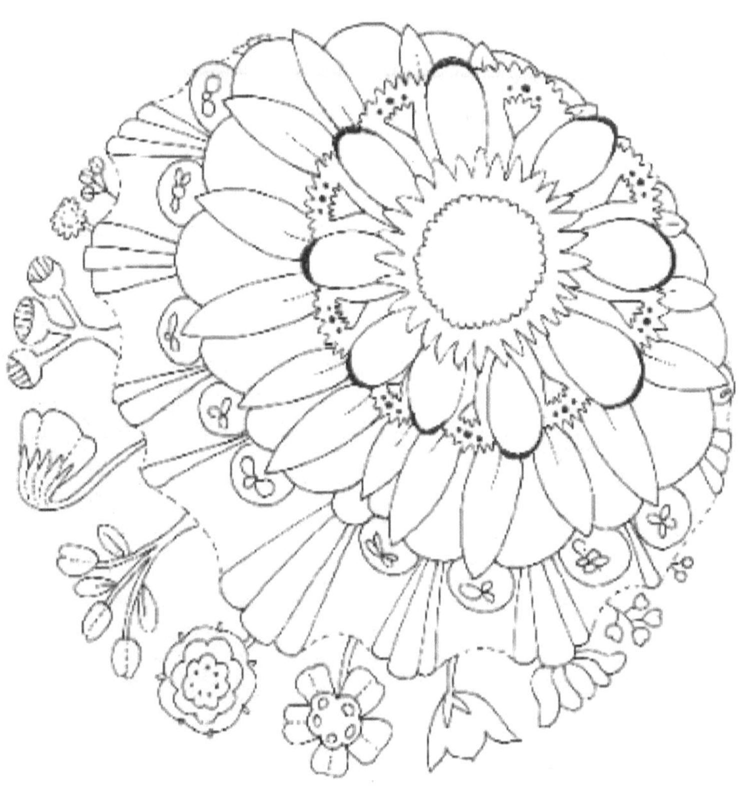

# Growing Up With Dolls

It takes courage to grow up
and become who you really are.
- *e. e. cummings* -

***

Before I opened my middle daughter's gift that Christmas morning, I already knew what it was. It had been a surprise the previous summer, when she first told me about it. Once I got over the shock, though, I had suggested she save it and give it to me for Christmas, by which time it would have faded from my memory and would seem virtually new again. This would save her from having to buy me another gift later on. (Some of us did this for our kids when they were very young; fair enough if we let them do it for us when we are old.) All I had asked was that she have it framed first.

I have always enjoyed a nice surprise, but when I was a child, if there was one thing I liked better than a surprise it was a doll. My allowance being as small as it was, the only occasions on which I was likely to get a new doll were either Christmas or my birthday. At such times, my brothers and I were each allowed to request one special gift.

Mom saved S&H Green Stamps - loyalty rewards you could collect by making purchases at selected grocery stores, pharmacies and gas stations. You would stick the stamps on the pages of the little book provided, and when the book was full, you could redeem it for merchandise from the S&H reward catalog. We had some idea of how much our parents were likely to spend (one child, one book), and we adjusted our desires accordingly. Later, we graduated to the Sears Roebuck Christmas catalog, the "Wish Book." Again, we managed to figure out how high the price ceiling was likely to be. I almost always wanted a doll.

I dreamed - sometimes really dreamed, like the time I woke up overjoyed, thinking my bedroom closet was full of dolls' shoes - of wardrobes for my dolls, not just the single outfits in which they arrived under the Christmas tree or next to the birthday cake. So I was always begging Mom to make doll clothes. Mom was a busy stay-at-home mother working hard at keeping up with four small children. A former school-district supervisor of music, she also helped my dad with his home business and taught piano lessons. She knew her way around a sewing machine and had all the tools and materials, but she just didn't enjoy sewing much. Music was her thing. And here was her only daughter, pulling at her sleeve and begging for doll clothes.

In desperation and with an eye to the future, she sat me down one day when I was about five at the dining room table, showed me how to thread a large darning needle and make a knot on the end of the thread, and taught me the running stitch. Her big shears were out of the question for me, but there was a smaller pair of "trimmers" in her sewing box that I could use. After giving instructions and watching for a few minutes to make reasonably sure I wouldn't poke myself in the eye, she went back to the kitchen to finish cooking supper. I settled in, planning to start with something small. How about a pair of panties? The doll I planned to sew for, my smallest, stood only a few inches high. You couldn't get a project much smaller than panties for that doll.

Having been introduced to the basic techniques, I learned quite a lot from that pilot sewing project. First, as my mom had made a point of explaining, you have to cut the garment big enough for seam allowances. Don't think you can just make the seam allowances narrower (or, shall we say, nonexistent) to compensate for a lack of planning in this regard. The second thing I learned was that a "big enough" seam allowance is bigger than you might think. Hence, the garment is going to look bigger to start with than you think it should.

Please don't think Mom had only *said* these things about seam allowances. She had demonstrated them as well, but I just didn't see how she could possibly be right. I was mistaken in this belief, as I found out as soon as I tried to squeeze my doll into that first pair of panties. (As some wise person once said, "Experience is not the best teacher, but it is the only one some people will listen to.") After shedding a few tears of frustration and losing all Mom's big needles (I kept dropping them on the floor and each time, instead of hunting for the lost needle, I would just get out another one; Mom finally said, "No more needles until you find the ones you dropped") I went back to work with a new respect for the outlandish rules of sewing.

Soon I had a wardrobe for my little doll, made up of...panties! A pair in every color of which my mom had a scrap of fabric. That doll may have had only one dress, but she had panties for every day of the week.

My next sewing teacher was Grandma, Mom's mother. Unlike Mom, she loved sewing. I was the only granddaughter, and when I was about seven, she decided I was old enough for more advanced lessons. First, she showed me her fabric stash, kept in a row of boxes neatly hidden behind a flowered curtain under a shelf in her "powder room." The last box at the end of the row, she told me, was *my* box; I could use any of that fabric whenever I wanted to. Surprise, surprise - I decided that what I really wanted to make first was a doll.

This ambitious project, scaled down to my ability level, had a plain muslin body, a sort-of-embroidered face, loops of yarn for hair, and a blue Hawaiian-print dress in that classic child's-first-sewing-project style: a rectangle with a hole cut out for the head, folded over and sewed up the sides. No sleeves, no hems. Not only did my newly-made doll not have an entire wardrobe, she didn't even have panties...all that early sewing experience, simply gone to waste. But she was the first doll I ever made, and I kept her for years.

At eight, I joined a local 4-H club as an associate member, which meant that my friend Sally's mom, the club Leader, let the two of us attend meetings and work on projects - usually sewing and cooking, in our city-based 4-H club - a year before we reached the minimum age, as long as we behaved ourselves. We were soon introduced to the sewing machine and began learning to sew outfits for ourselves as well as for our dolls.

By this time dolls, sewing, and reading books were three of my favorite things. When they all came together, how special was that? I spent hours at the library, where I soon discovered books on doll-making that I could read and understand. One in particular, *The Doll Book* by Estelle Ansley Worrell, was filled with historical information about American styles of the past, with a section of patterns printed in the back of the book to trace off for an entire family of costume dolls and their clothes.

I borrowed this book from the library again and again, even taking it with me to Grandma's house the next time my brothers and I spent the week with her. When I asked her, Grandma was more than willing to help me work on a project from the book. We chose a doll and an outfit, but ran into a snag: no matter how we hunted through the pattern pages, we couldn't find the sleeve for the dress I wanted. I was not only disappointed, but annoyed. Everyone knew that sewing patterns were created by professionals using techniques unknown to ordinary mortals, and since we had no way of contacting the professional who had created this one, we were out of luck. Impatiently, I waited for Grandma to suggest I choose another design. Instead, she said, "We'll just have to make a sleeve pattern ourselves."

From the bodice pattern, she took a few casual measurements; she drew a few lines on a piece of paper. A sleeve pattern, looking remarkably professional, appeared before my wondering eyes, and when we cut out the little dress and sewed it up, *the sleeve fit.* How did Grandma know how to do that? It would be years before I dared to try such a thing myself, but I didn't forget.[4]

By the time I was 10, most of my friends were leaving dolls behind, turning their attention to the current boy bands, light romantic fiction or Avon's collection of scented bath products. In my opinion, they were hurrying into the grown-ups' world much too soon. But impending maturity has a way of catching up with all of us, and soon it would catch up even with me.

The year I was 11, my older brother got a brass wind-up alarm clock as a Christmas gift. This was something I never would have thought of asking for. Now, I wanted one. Or did I want what it represented? It wasn't a toy; it belonged to the grown-up world in some indefinable way that made it "cool." I thought back over the presents my brothers and I had received that day and realized Eric's all had this sophisticated, grown-up quality. I decided to ask Mom and Dad about it.

"Why does Eric get cooler gifts than the rest of us?"

It must have been an unexpected question from a kid who up till now had never asked for anything but a doll, and I got an unexpected answer.

"That's easy. He doesn't ask for what he wants; he lets us choose for him."

I spent the next year chewing this thought over. When the Sears "Wish Book" arrived at our house that fall, I leafed through it and picked out my favorites, as usual, but made a point of not registering any requests. This was an experiment, I decided. I would wait and see what my parents would choose for me if I said nothing.

Then it was Christmas morning again. In our family, Christmas tradition, like other traditions, was occasionally subject to the element of surprise. For example, you knew you could rush downstairs before the parents were up and explore the contents of your filled Christmas stocking right away, but you had to wait till the family had assembled before you touched anything else, and then it had to be done decently and in order. The times it was hardest to wait were the years when Christmas fell on a Sunday. Dad was the choir director at our church and a Christmas Sunday service was special, an event not to be missed. On those Christmas Sundays, we were, as usual, allowed to check out our stockings before church, but the rest of the presents would have to wait. To make up for the nearly unbearable suspense we were thus forced to endure, we might find something unusual waiting for us at home on a Christmas Sunday.

Although this wasn't a Christmas-on-Sunday year, when we came downstairs that morning we found that Dad and Mom had set up a treasure hunt, with clues for each kid leading to a special present. I finally tracked down a thin, flat package with my name on it behind my dad's desk in his office. When I unwrapped it, I discovered that my parents had bought me my own copy of *The Doll Book*.

I still own a copy of this book. My first artist sales would include dolls I had made from this book's patterns. There was the time, for example, when at 15 I came home from a week-long visit with friends to find that my parents had sold one of my costume dolls while I was gone. One of my dad's business associates, a collector, had seen it displayed on the mantel, asked about it and made an offer, Dad and Mom explained rather sheepishly, handing me the money.

"We thought you wouldn't mind. We figured you could make another one, if you wanted to."

I was so astonished that a grown-up would pay what seemed to me a breathtaking sum for something I had made that I didn't even mind that my parents had agreed to the transaction without asking me first. They were right - I knew I could always make another one just like it if I wanted to. Imagine my doll in a collection!

I finished school, married, raised a family, made dolls for my own children, for other family members, for friends, occasionally selling one. After our youngest son started school, I decided to begin treating dollmaking as a business rather than just a hobby that sometimes helped finance my arts and crafts habit. I got interested in using papier-mâché for the dolls' heads, and in line with skills I had developed as a portrait artist, I began experimenting with dolls that looked more like real people.

When our middle daughter told me she would be going to the 2011 North American Discworld convention in Madison, Wisconsin, where she was going to personally meet British author Sir Terry Pratchett, I made a gift to send him: a doll based on Captain Sam Vimes, a favorite character from his fantasy/humor Discworld book series. Sir Terry had said once that he envisioned this character as resembling well-known British actor Pete Postlethwaite. I found pictures of the actor online, created a papier-mâché head based on him as a model, painted the features as I thought Rembrandt might have, added a wig and a stuffed fabric body and then dressed him according to the descriptions in the book series. I didn't know if the author would even accept a gift from a fan, but it was worth a try.

My daughter returned from the convention to report that Sir Terry had not only received the doll with surprise and pleasure, but immediately and correctly identified the character it represented. (All of his fans knew by this time that the author was suffering from a rare form of early-onset Alzheimer's.)

"It's Sam Vimes, isn't it?" he asked as my daughter placed the doll in his arms. "What? It's for me to keep? Thank you!"

On Christmas morning, I unwrapped my gift to find an ornamental metal frame holding a card with Terry Pratchett's autograph scribbled across it. He had signed his name on hundreds of these cards in the weeks before the convention so as to leave him more time and energy at the event for his fans. The autographs were for registered guests, but he had pulled an extra one off the pile and given it to my daughter for me, to thank me for the Sam Vimes doll. What a gift! It was something I never would have thought to ask for - and if there's anything I enjoy more than a doll nowadays, it's a nice surprise.

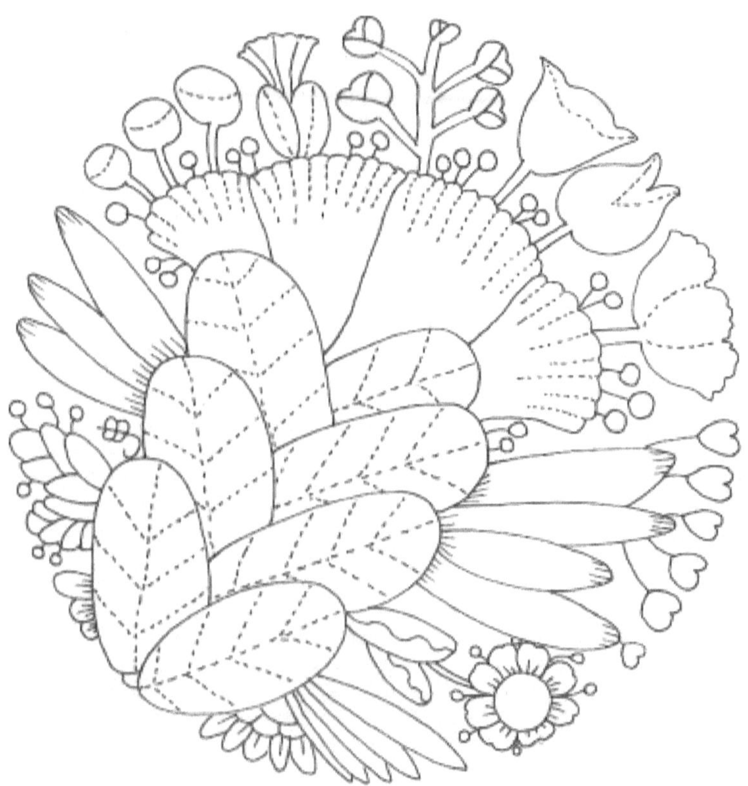

# Spinning My Wheels

(I)t is the law of all progress that it is made
by passing through some stages of instability—
and that it may take a very long time.
- *Teilhard de Chardin* -

---

Spinning wool on a spinning wheel is more than just a way to turn out yarn. For me, the small, rhythmic, repetitive motions make for a comforting leisure activity similar to having a cup of coffee or watching a favorite movie after a long day of work. With most other leisure activities, you don't have yarn to show for it afterward. On the other hand, becoming an experienced hand-spinner makes it possible to enjoy coffee *and* a movie *and* still end up with yarn - the best kind of multitasking.

My grandmother told me once that I should have been born 100 years earlier than I was. From childhood, I was fascinated by old ways, old tools, old methods of doing things. (I drew the line at outhouses, although I found I could take even these in my stride when I lived for a while in a remote location with no indoor plumbing.)

I collected souvenirs that made me feel connected to those olden days. The first time I went on a school trip to a historical re-enactment museum, I came home with homemade cinnamon-scented soap from the gift shop. I saved it for years, using it only occasionally - treasuring its look, its feel, the fact of its existence as well as its distinctive fragrance. The next time I visited such a museum, I bought a little coin purse made from fabric hand-woven on one of the museum's looms. Then my older brother (who also went on school trips to museums) gave me a ring fashioned from an iron nail hand-forged and bent in a circle on a blacksmith's anvil, which I thought was pretty cool. But for some reason, with soapmaking and weaving and blacksmithing I was willing to enjoy the end result while admiring the process from a distance. With spinning, I wanted to get in there and participate.

How does a person go about learning an archaic craft? This was the early 1970s, I was a teenager, and I didn't yet know anything about the do-it-yourself, self-sufficient back-to-the land movement that had been gaining momentum for a decade at that point. I did have a library card, so the library was where I went first, not expecting to get much help there. To my astonishment, the library had several books on handspinning. The how-to-manual-artfully-disguised-as-a-story I ended up taking home with me that day was *The Joy of Spinning* by Marilyn Kluger. Ms. Kluger, like me, was fascinated by spinning. Her story began when, as a child, she had seen her grandmother spin wool, and her interest in the craft revived when as an adult she too visited a historical site and watched a spinning demonstration.

By the time I'd gotten halfway through the book, *I* wanted a spinning wheel of my own, but in those days you couldn't just walk into a yarn shop and buy one, as you can do in my town now. In those days, old ones in good condition were rare, new ones almost impossible to find. It had taken Ms. Kluger months to track down a working model for herself, nor when I first decided to learn had I ever seen one in use outside a museum.

But times were changing. Only a couple of years later, my mom would be able to order a brand-new spinning wheel from the Ashford company in New Zealand. Ashfords are now among the most popular spinning wheels in the world, commonly available in many a yarn shop as well as at fiber festivals and online, but my mom's arrived in the form of a kit, the pieces of which had to be given a wood finish, then assembled by the owner.

Meanwhile, my first step toward becoming a spinner was with the most basic of yarn-making tools: a hand-held or "drop" spindle, fashioned for me by a woodworking family friend. Until about 1500 years ago, when the first prototypical spinning wheels were invented somewhere in middle Asia, all the yarn or thread anyone ever created was spun on variants of the drop spindle, and there are societies that continue to use them to this day. They're simple and inexpensive to make (mine was a foot-long dowel weighted at the bottom by a cylindrical block of hard maple) and very portable, but their simplicity is deceptive.

How would I describe my first few days of learning to use the drop spindle? Frustrating, that's how. To begin with, I had no wool. I was a city kid who had never seen a sheep up close, let alone handled raw wool fiber, and I had no idea how to find any. (How did we ever get things done before the Internet? Better find out, in case we need to do it again someday.) I had been sewing costume dolls for several years, though, so I used what I had, which was polyester fiberfill - a big bag of stuffing. Talk about a crossover between ancient and modern technology, but it looked (enough) like wool to me. I guessed it would probably work.

For the second time in my life, I shed tears over a craft process. Here I was, reasonably good with any handcraft I had ever tried. I had been successfully making things for at least a decade at age-appropriate skill levels. I could draw, paint, sew, knit, fabricate various art objects from paper, but spinning was - well, a different ball of fluff, so to speak. I'd pull off a handful of fiber, fluff it out. Lay fluffed-out fiber in hand next to fluffed-out fiber on end of "leader," a length of yarn tied to spindle to help spinner get started. Grasp the two bits of fluffed-out fiber together between fingers, hoping to convince them to be friends forever. Give spindle an energetic twirl in midair, then...quick! While it was still spinning, try to pull out enough fluff from both bits to twist together...hurry! The strand of yarn I was creating lengthened...the whirling, dangling spindle inched lower, lower...*It's going to work this time, I just know it.* But already the momentum had begun to slow, then reverse. Before I could grab for the untwisting yarn, it had pulled apart. I'd hear the crack of the wooden spindle hitting the floor. (Again.) More tears.

"Fiber slippage." This, I learned, was the technical term for the problem I couldn't seem to conquer. I had also discovered why, on the most elemental level, it is called a "drop" spindle. But two or three days of determined if tearful practice yielded a few yards of real yarn. *Polyester* yarn, to be fair; sections of very thick and very thin yarn, some parts resembling tightly wound wire while others were barely cohesive, the texture of the yarn shifting from one to the other with disconcerting frequency. I saved my first yarn for a long time. I used to haul it out to show to new spinners later on who, discouraged by fiber slippage and dropping spindles, were saying they thought they would never "get it."

When I did eventually get hold of some sheep's wool, I was enchanted by the contrast between it and my polyester stuffing. Texture is what makes the difference. A polyester fiber looks like a smooth tube when viewed under a microscope; a wool fiber looks like a tube made of tiny, scaly pinecones. Because of its smoothness, you have to coax polyester to stick together when spinning, but most wool fibers, when spun, will naturally cling to each other. The tiny, overlapping pinecone-like scales *want* to bring each other along when wool fluff is stretched out and twisted, much like a teenage girl at the lake who doesn't want to get her hair wet and grabs one or more of her friends when someone tries to pull her off the raft. This tendency to stick together makes sheep's wool one of the easiest of the fibers to spin.

Even before my mother ordered her own Ashford kit from New Zealand, the family friend who had made my drop spindle, intrigued by an archaic craft, had started work on a design for a functional spinning wheel he'd found in a modern woodworking magazine. The one he built that eventually appeared in my living room would within a few days reveal its own idiosyncrasies and quirks. (All spinning wheels, no matter how new or well-made, tend to have idiosyncrasies and quirks. It's something about moving parts, especially wooden ones; they give a mechanical device personality.) Soon I was turning out yarn on it. Without so many tears this time, because by now not only did I have some real wool, I had experience.

Once you get the feel of spinning, it becomes almost automatic. Yarn thickness begins to even out as you match the rhythm of the wheel with the quality of the wool you're using. It becomes so automatic, so relaxing, that you may find yourself falling asleep over the wheel, as I have done. Thick-and-thin "artisanal" yarn will after a few days of practice be hard to produce, even if you want to, and you'll find that many non-spinners have a hard time believing it is handspun if it isn't thick-and-thin. Plying (twisting two or more spun strands, or "plies," together to make a stronger yarn) and dyeing are further refinements of the yarn-making process, and most spinners will eventually experiment with them. And then what?

To knit, crochet or weave yarn you spun yourself is like taking the scenic route to work. To continue to the next step - to use or give a finished product that started off in your hands as mere fluff - is like reaching the end of a long journey, the top of a high mountain with a great view, or a destination you've dreamed about all your life. You look at where you are now and then back at the tiny, slow steps that got you there and it just makes you feel good to think about it all. Every time you throw that shawl over your shoulders, carry that handwoven bag, or see someone else wearing that cap you crocheted for them out of yarn you yourself made, you get to enjoy it all over again. I confess that I've even daydreamed of one day raising my own sheep in hopes of providing myself with wool for my own use, thus taking my fondness for this ancient fibercraft a step further.

For now, though, I'm content for spinning to remain a pleasant pastime - my cup of coffee, my favorite movie, my gently rising path to the heights where there's a really great view. The kind of leisure activity I not only enjoy in the moment, but continue to treasure the results of long afterward.

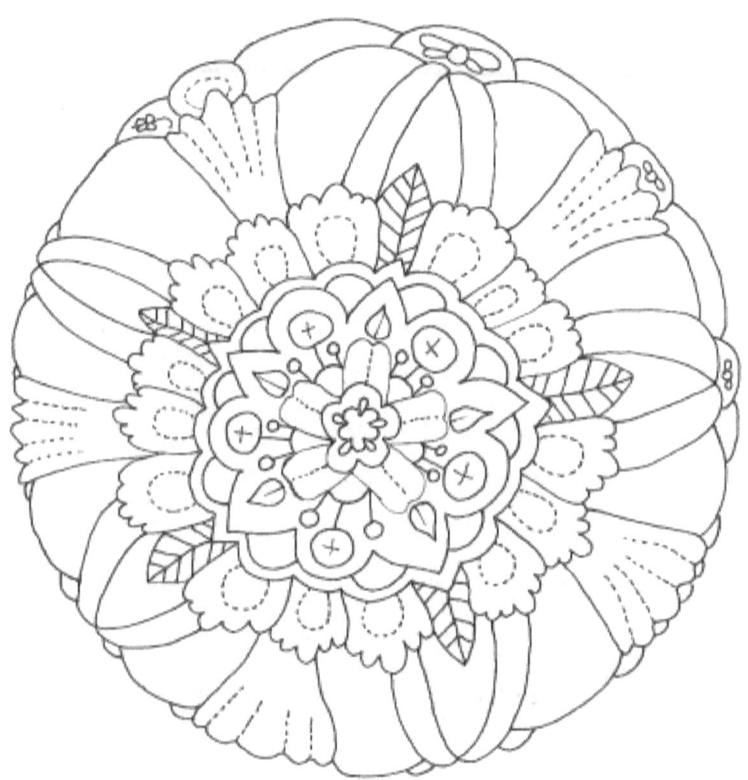

# Fried As You Like It

Eating connects us to our histories
as much as it connects our souls to our bodies,
our bodies to the earth.
*- Evan D. G. Fraser -*

Jet lag. Culture shock. Seven months pregnant and balancing a squirming toddler on my nonexistent lap (in the days before mandatory child safety seats in cars) while packed with my husband and four other adults into a minivan that looked to be not much larger than a North American six-seater sedan but had almost enough room in the back for our luggage, traveling cross-country for a day that had, for me, already seemingly lasted about 24 hours and wasn't nearly over yet, I experienced my first Japanese restaurant meal at noon, local time: a combination of chicken, egg and vegetables served over rice and called, somewhat unnervingly, "parent and child bowl" - the "parent" being the chicken, and the "child" being the egg.

The owner of the minivan was a friend we had met when he was visiting our hometown in Canada. He and his brother had kindly agreed to pick us up at the airport, since they had the largest car. He and our American missionary sponsor, whose English classes we had come to help teach so she could travel when necessary, had put their heads together when it was time to stop for lunch, and they decided that "parent and child bowl" was likely the kind of dish newcomers to Japan would find tolerable.

Well, I tolerated it. It was food. I was hungry...I was *pregnant;* of course I was hungry. I ate it. It wasn't disgusting. I would never again order it in a restaurant, but it was what there was, that day. Oh, and did I mention that I had not yet mastered the art of using chopsticks? What had I been thinking before I left Canada?

Much later, when I had learned how to make the "parent and child bowl," *oyako domburi,* I found to my surprise that I liked it after all. Living in Japan for a couple of years eventually broke down my North American resistance to many foods that seemed strange when I was first confronted by them, but which were, in fact, made mostly from ingredients that were really not all that different from things I had cooked and eaten on my home turf.

I would come to enjoy (and learn to cook) many of these foods, to the point that I would long for them when we returned to Canada, then moved to upper east Tennessee later on; and I would be delighted when I found their more specialized ingredients in Asian grocery stores here. Eventually, many of these Japanese ingredients would be stocked in the "ethnic" sections of ordinary North American grocery stores, as more people on this side of the Pacific Ocean began to realize what they had been missing out on.

Meanwhile, during our first few weeks in Japan I was still figuring out how to conform to the different ways of our new home. We took turns cooking meals in the house we shared with several Japanese and American missionaries. Our diet was a mixture of Asian and Western cuisine; as often as not, the Japanese cooks prepared American-style food, and the American cooks served Japanese dishes, and as with the "parent and child bowl"

I had encountered the first day, I found some of it took getting used to. Soup served at the beginning of every meal, made with fish broth and seaweed... Fermented soybeans that were mucilaginous, like okra, served with beaten raw egg and chopped scallions over rice...What had I been expecting? Hamburgers? I had been taught as a child to eat a little of everything without making a fuss, so I didn't go hungry even if what there was to eat wasn't always top of my list of favorites. Slowly, I began to get used to our varied menu.

Then one day my husband and I had to go shopping for something for which we needed an interpreter. One of our Japanese missionary friends agreed to come along to help, and when it was time for lunch she asked us if we had ever had *okonomi yaki*.

"What?"

She led us to a restaurant on the ground floor of the grocery/ department store where we were shopping, and ordered a large one for the three of us to share. Thus I was introduced to my first favorite Japanese food.

*Okonomi yaki,* which can be loosely translated "fried-as-you-like-it," has also been called "Japanese pizza," and with good reason. Although it's really a pancake made primarily of shredded cabbage in an egg and flour batter, it sort of looks like pizza when served. Like pizza in America, it is also a popular restaurant or street food for which customers can choose their own ingredients, some of which are incorporated into the mixture during the cooking process, while other toppings are added just before eating, at the table.

*Okonomi yaki* may start with cabbage, egg and flour, but it doesn't usually stop there, any more than pizza usually stops with a bread-dough crust and tomato sauce. Since leaving the isolated region of Japan where we lived for two years, I have discovered that *okonomi yaki* is made differently in different parts of the country. While it originated in the more southern parts of Japan (Osaka and Hiroshima), the recipe I share here is the way I was taught to make it in the out-of-the way coastal region where we lived, near the Japan Sea. This recipe came from my friend Kimie, who introduced us to it, and whose father was a chef. Well, this is *mostly* the way she taught me to make it. I may have Americanized it, just a little...

One egg per serving is beaten with as much flour as needed to make a thick, pancake-like batter. Then other ingredients are mixed in. The main one - shredded cabbage - is usually joined by thinly sliced onions or scallions, often both. After that comes one of the most important of the traditional ingredients: shredded red pickled ginger root, *beni shōga*. The thin scarlet streaks visible on the surface of the pancake give the white and pale green cabbage-egg-and-onion batter a nice visual pop as well as the hint of bright, hot ginger that - along with the cabbage and onions - also makes this dish smell so delicious while it is cooking. This fragrance is further enhanced by the addition of a little garlic, either in the form of garlic powder or granules, or whole fresh garlic, smashed and minced.

Many other vegetables can also be included, and this is where the "as you like it" aspect comes in. Here in North America, when I'm in a hurry I often just throw in some frozen mixed vegetables - corn, green beans, peas, diced carrots and sometimes lima beans. I've also recently begun adding chopped cilantro, called *mitsuba* ("three-leaf") in Japan.

At this point, except for the egg used to make the batter, this could be an all-plant-based dish, but many cooks add additional protein, either meat or seafood. The first choice in Kimie's version would have been thinly sliced roast pork, a staple in many Japanese dishes. After that, seafood is a good choice - shrimp, crab, squid - while smoked salmon is quite luxurious. When we're at home in North America I have used thinly shredded ham, cooked bacon, or even luncheon meat such as bologna or hot dogs cut in julienne strips, although this is not at all traditional and will definitely give your "Japanese pizza" an American flair.

If you happen to have small amounts of any leftover stir-fried or tempura vegetables, meats or seafood, these can be thinly sliced and added as well. Even the little deep-fried batter particles that separate from the larger pieces when cooking tempura can be saved and stirred into *okonomi yaki;* they will taste like whatever was cooked in the batter. In Japan, shops that served tempura would sometimes sell these leftover particles by the bagful at the end of the day. You could buy them then and add them to your own dishes at home.

Bear in mind that the two main ingredients for this dish are the egg and flour batter and the shredded cabbage, of which the bulk of the mixture will consist. Of the other ingredients you will need only small quantities.

*Okonomi yaki* is cooked on an oiled griddle or in a frying pan, much like a pancake. It can be made into one large cake, like the one my husband and I shared with Kimie that day in the department-store restaurant; or several smaller ones, which is what I usually do as they are quicker and easier to cook. It may be covered with a lid for the first part of the cooking process to help the top "set." Give it enough time to cook all the way through, flipping several times until it is a rich golden brown on both sides. Serve right away with a selection of condiments and garnishes (again, "as you like it") such as soy sauce, Worcestershire sauce, ketchup, mayonnaise, ground black or white sesame seed, toasted and shredded *nori* - the dark green seaweed sold in papery sheets which is often wrapped around sushi - and, if possible, dried and shaved bonito, an ocean fish. This dried fish, *katsuoboshi*, adds an interesting element to your freshly-cooked *okonomi yaki*; it may look like thin curls of wood shavings, but when it is sprinkled on top of the hot pancake, the rising steam makes the shavings wiggle and curl in the most lifelike way. Even I don't understand why I, mildly disturbed by something called "mother and child bowl" on my first day in Japan, have never minded eating this garnish that acts as if it was still alive. Nevertheless, it is one of the things I miss most when I make *okonomi yaki* in North America, since it is hard to find where I live now.

*Basic Okonomi Yaki*

Serves one. May be multiplied as desired.

For the batter:

● 1 egg mixed with enough flour to make a thick batter, as for pancakes. If you are cooking for a group and need to economize on eggs, use fewer eggs and add a little water. About ¼ cup of water replaces one large egg.

● Garlic powder and salt to taste.

Slice or shred finely and add:

● A cup or more of cabbage. I was originally taught to use raw cabbage, but was told that some cooks steam it lightly first, and I have found we prefer it this way. It's up to you; remember, "as you like it!"

● About a quarter of a cup of onions, scallions, or a combination of the two

Add a couple of tablespoonfuls of shredded red pickled ginger *(beni shōga).*

You may also add, *in small amounts,* your choice of:

● cooked corn, broccoli or cauliflower, green beans, shredded zucchini or summer squash, shredded carrots, shredded white or sweet potatoes, a little chopped fresh cilantro, etc.

● other shredded greens: kale, collards, spinach, chard

● leftover stir-fried or tempura vegetables

● anything else you can think of that sounds good.

Any vegetables which are not already in small pieces should be thinly sliced, or shredded julienne-style.

For protein, try small amounts of one or more of the following:

● small pieces of thinly sliced roast pork

● chopped cooked seafood: shrimp, crab, squid

● smoked salmon

- sliced or crumbled cooked bacon

- thinly sliced bits of ham or (if you must) other processed luncheon meats.

Stir well. At this point, your mixture may look like coleslaw with thick mayonnaise dressing. There should be enough batter to hold the other ingredients together when it is cooked. You can thin it with a little water, add more flour to thicken it, or shred and stir in more vegetables, after you have cooked the first trial cake and can see whether or not it needs adjusting.

Heat a lightly greased griddle or frying pan as if you were going to make pancakes. Spoon mounds of *okonomi yaki* mixture onto the hot pan. You may cover the pan with a lid (a domed pot lid, if you are using a griddle) to hold the heat in and cook the top of the cake faster. After a few minutes, uncover and check the underside of each cake. If it is nicely browned, flip the cake and press it down hard with the back of the metal spatula to flatten it so it cooks through. Cook till the second side is well browned. When you press down with the metal spatula, no raw batter should ooze out the top or sides; if it does, cook it a little longer. The cake can be turned several times until you are satisfied with the doneness level.

Serve immediately or cover and keep warm in the oven, on a warming zone or in a slow cooker.

At the table, pass garnishes with which each person can decorate their own "Japanese pizza:"

- soy and Worcestershire sauce

- other sauces used in Asian cooking, such as wasabi

- ketchup

- mayonnaise

- ground white or black sesame seeds

- toasted, shredded *nori*. The Japanese kind is sold in square sheets in a cellophane envelope and comes already scored. Toast it lightly by holding it over an open flame or a stove burner for a few seconds, break or cut it with scissors along the score lines, and then cut it into smaller pieces about 1/8" wide.

- *katsuoboshi* - if you can find some (lucky you!)

The best way to serve *okonomi yaki* is for one person to assume the position of cook, offering the cakes fresh off the griddle as guests are ready for them. However, if you are serving a large crowd, it may be better to fry enough cakes ahead of time for everyone to start eating at once, keeping them warm as described above. Then you can add fresh ones as you go along.

*Okonomi yaki* is street food, often prepared and served from open-air grills, but once when we were visiting in a large city in Japan, a friend took our family to an *okonomi yaki* restaurant. We sat, Japanese style, on a slightly raised platform around a low table with a griddle built into the center. Customers could order their "as you like it" ingredients from the menu, then have it cooked right there in front of them by a restaurant employee, or - if they wanted to - they could cook it themselves. Since we had small children with us, our friend requested that our *okonomi yaki* be cooked in the kitchen and brought to us ready to eat. I did see other customers in the restaurant cooking their own and it looked like fun. If I go back to Japan, I would like to visit one of those restaurants again and try my hand at cooking my own "Japanese pizza" that way.

Here follows a recipe for an even quicker, more Americanized version of this dish:

*Practically Instant Okonomi Yaki*

Make the basic egg and flour batter as shown above. Then add:

• pre-packaged coleslaw mix (red and green cabbage, grated carrots)

• thinly sliced onions (could use pre-packaged, frozen, or dehydrated)

• *Beni shōga,* or grated raw ginger root, or a bit of powdered ginger

• a little garlic powder and salt to taste

Stir in:

• a few frozen mixed vegetables

• pre-cooked bacon bits

• small amounts of any thinly sliced leftovers you might have in the fridge (see first recipe for suggested vegetables and meats)

Cook and serve as described above.

The following is yet another variant on real Japanese *okonomi yaki*. I may be wrong about this, but I suspect before I invented it last fall it had never been done before. Try it when you're going to a potluck and you want to bring something a little unusual.

*"Babycakes" Okonomi Yaki Pops*

Follow the standard procedure, but prepare the batter by stirring instant pancake mix instead of plain flour into the beaten eggs, and shred or chop vegetables and other ingredients very, very finely. Cook in cake-pop baker till done. Add lollipop sticks if desired. Serve these little globular *okonomi yaki* with or without the standard dipping sauces.

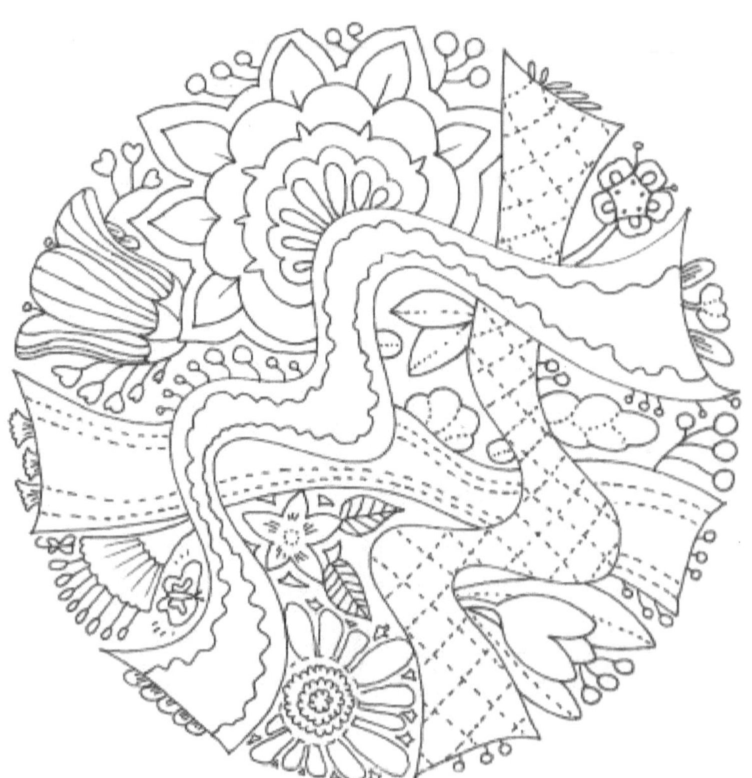

# Clay: The Forgiving Medium

(C)reative projects, especially larger projects,
don't happen overnight. It takes working at it in a series
of moments consistently. It also reminds us that a career,
a portfolio, or even a hobby takes time to build.
Every project you complete is a step closer
to becoming great at what you do.
*- Benjamin Barnhart -*

When we put things on a "bucket list," they are often things we have dreamed of doing but aren't sure we'll ever get a chance at. You know, stuff like climbing Mount Everest. Or getting a part in a Broadway musical. (Maybe even just *seeing* a Broadway musical, on Broadway.) Or meeting a celebrity we've always admired. Or traveling to the Faroe Islands to interview the head of tourism and the shepherds, and maybe pet the sheep, who created their own "Google Sheep View" at a time when Google had informed them they weren't important enough to qualify for the ordinary view other people's streets were getting.

Working in clay was not very high on my bucket list. It wasn't that I didn't want to do it - the look, feel, and idea of handmade pottery have always appealed to me. It was that I knew the craft was, financially and logistically, out of my reach.

Creating things out of clay may seem pretty simple. What is clay, after all, but a special kind of mud? Well, it is and it isn't. Clay for pottery may be relatively common and inexpensive, but there is more to it than just mud, and potters all the way back to prehistoric times have been adding various substances to their clay to make it stronger and more workable. More than that, the process that changes clay into pottery requires the use of a kiln. *Greenware* - unfired pottery - will return to its original state, a special kind of mud, when exposed to water.

I didn't have a kiln or any way of accessing one, but as a dollmaker some years ago I'd been interested in finding a basic, inexpensive, hard-surface material to experiment with - something that didn't need firing at high temperatures - for a more realistic doll's head. Eventually, my explorations led me to papier-mâché. This material, which can be made at home from scratch and also comes in an instant version from art and craft suppliers, shares many of the qualities of clay without clay's drawbacks for a kitchen-table hobbyist. Papier-mâché in pulp form can be modeled like clay, but is much lighter in weight and far less fragile; it uses commonly available materials, requires no firing, and once dry can be sanded, cut, glued and painted like wood. It has been used as prop material in theaters and the film industry for decades. Following online tutorials, I spent several years making dolls' heads in papier-mâché and found it a simple and rewarding medium. Then we moved to a town where the local Senior Center had a clay studio.

By this time I qualified as a senior citizen; the cost of membership was reasonable, and - equally important - kilns, potter's wheels and workspace were all provided by the Center. All we had to buy was our clay, glazes, and hand tools. I signed up for a beginners' pottery class, and a dream I had cherished only very, very distantly began to be fulfilled.

Clay turned out to have a lot of surprises. To start with, for a substance that shared many qualities with ordinary mud, it could be a bit of a prima donna, requiring (with some exceptions) a very light touch. Then, for all its celebrated workability, a clay piece had "memory." Once it had been shaped a certain way and begun to dry, it might insist on reverting to that shape when you weren't looking, even if it still felt flexible and you had decided you wanted to tweak it a little. Furthermore, although a piece had to be bone-dry before it could go into the kiln, if it dried too fast it might crack before you ever got it there. It was wise to set a drying piece of greenware on a shelf far away from air currents, covering it with newspaper or plastic and checking on it regularly to make sure it was on schedule based on what you wanted to do with it.

Another surprise (and this was a good one) was that right up till it was fired, clay was endlessly recyclable. A piece that was damaged while still wet could be re-worked right away. A broken, warped, or otherwise unsatisfactory piece of bone-dry greenware could be soaked in water to reduce it to mud, spread out to dry again till it reached the right consistency, then kneaded, or *wedged*, to turn it back into fresh clay. A friend in the clay room said it well when she remarked that as an artistic medium, clay was one of the most forgiving. Even once-fired *(bisque)* pottery can be crushed to powder (fired, crushed pottery is called *grog*) and added to a fresh batch of moist clay to make the finished product stronger. Although we do not have the equipment for this procedure in our Senior Center studio, the ready-to-use clay we buy does contain grog. I've often wondered whose fired-and-crushed pottery has been mixed into *my* clay to make my pottery more durable. Or do manufacturers fire pottery scraps on purpose, then pulverize them and add them in? I'm sure my supplier would tell me, if I asked a few questions.

The one thing about working in clay that I hadn't been expecting, though, was the good mood I always enjoyed while doing it. I noticed that I always returned home from a day in the clay room feeling cheerful and optimistic, ready to take on whatever other challenges life might present. Naturally, there's the psychological uplift of working in a medium one enjoys, and the pleasure of being creative, but I began to wonder if it had something to do with handling the clay itself. Take gardening, for example: research indicates that gardening can be a mood-booster - there's something about having earth on your hands that is beneficial for the human brain. Is it possible that clay, an earth-based substance, has a similar positive effect on those who work with it?

Or maybe it's just the aspect of *control* that is so relaxing. Clay may be a prima donna, but once you understand its limitations and are willing to work with them, you can usually figure out a way to get what you want from it. Among job descriptions, experts have discovered, the most stressful kind of work is the kind with a high ratio of responsibility to control. If you are expected to perform to a high standard without having much control over the outcome, that's what creates stress. The lowest-stress work is the kind that gives the worker the most autonomy over his finished product. Clay gives you that kind of control. At least I thought it did till I decided I needed to learn to use the potter's wheel.

I attempted to learn *throwing* (making vessels on the potters' wheel) several times, with different teachers but without success, before finally achieving a kind of basic proficiency thanks to two semesters of ceramics classes in college. Watching others struggle with the wheel, and observing the refreshing honesty of teachers who made a point of showing us their mistakes and how to fix (or discard) a piece unexpectedly gone wonky, helped me confront and defeat my fear that I would never, ever master this skill.

It helped a lot to have access to unlimited amounts of endlessly recyclable clay. The college ceramics studio had a *pug mill* - a motorized device like a giant sausage grinder, strong enough to churn up assorted wet and dry clay scraps and squeeze the newly mixed clay out in giant-sausage-like chunks for re-use. Any assigned project that just wasn't living up to expectations (or suddenly changed its fickle mind about the destiny you had planned for it, after an hour of careful labor on the wheel) could be chucked into the *reclaim* bin, from which it would eventually go through the pug mill and be trundled back out into the studio as fresh clay, ready for a second chance at immortality. (As my first teacher once told us when she was doing a demo on the potter's wheel, "It may fight you...but you're going to win in the end.")

Today, I'm looking forward to a day in the clay studio. The feel of the clay, the pleasant anticipation of making something I want or need, the quiet atmosphere (even with other potters in the room, it seldom gets noisy in there) and above all the absorbing interest of seeing my project slowly take shape under my hands, make for a very peaceful environment. A little music in the background adds to the ambience of this art form with its prehistoric origins. I always go home refreshed from a day of making pottery, and I don't even mind that it took me so many years to get around to trying it, because now I'm making up for lost time.

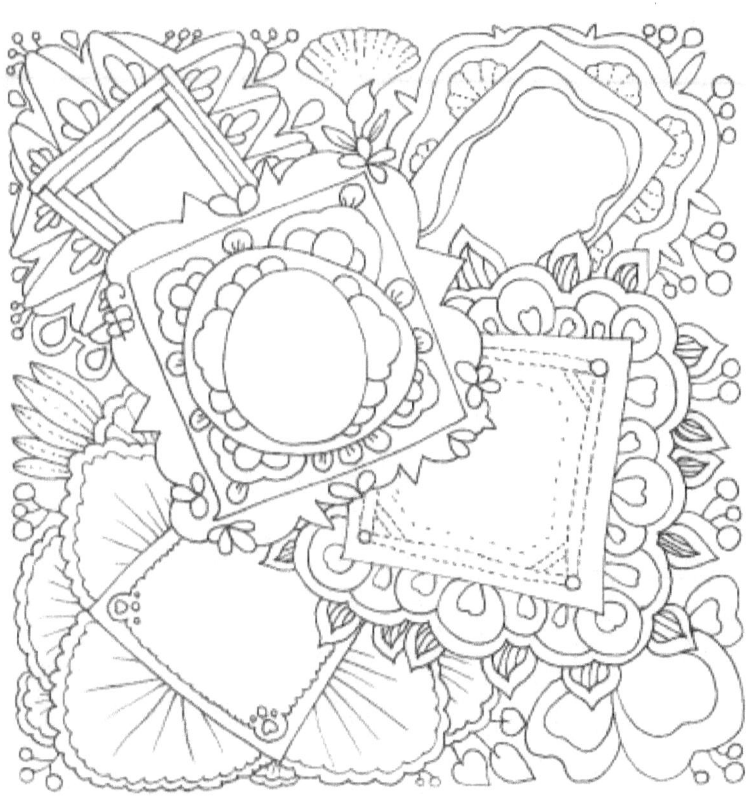

# The Day I Cried in College

Life is like an onion; you peel it off one layer at a time,
and sometimes you weep.
*Carl Sandberg*

---

As an artist, I often tell people that one of the scariest things I do on a regular basis is to walk into a shop, show my art to the proprietor and ask if they are willing to sell it. I've talked myself into doing this scary thing many times, but it's still nerve-wracking. One of the scariest things I have ever done in my life, though, was to walk into our local community college and ask for directions to the registration office. On my last day of high school more than forty years earlier, I had walked out promising myself I would never have to set foot in a classroom again.

It hadn't always been like that. Like most kids, I'd spent the first few years of school learning to read, write, do basic addition and subtraction, and get along with other kids on the playground. These were challenges I could handle, and if I ever thought about my place in the educational system at all, I thought of myself as a good student.

*"Barbie daydreams."* The note my teacher had written on my third-grade report card stared back at me. Suddenly, I had a mental image of myself as my teacher must see me: sitting at my little desk, chin on hand, eyes on the drifting clouds, while the rest of the class - the non-daydreamers - paid close attention to the

newly-introduced multiplication tables. I was mortified. I *daydreamed* - apparently, a serious enough fault that my parents needed to be informed. It was the first time I'd gotten negative feedback on a report card, although in retrospect I realize it might have been no more than an observation. (This teacher would, later on, recommend me for an experimental, accelerated program in another school.) At any rate, I interpreted her written comment as criticism - so, I seem to remember, did my parents, who upon seeing the note suggested gently that I pay better attention in class.

I would struggle with concentration issues as long as I was in school, and sometimes I failed to pick up on important information because of it. Math in particular had a hard time holding my interest, although I always got passing grades. But it wasn't only math.

There was, for example, the time my sixth-grade teacher spent an afternoon explaining the outline method of taking notes. Somehow I got distracted, missed a step right at the beginning, and was hopelessly lost for the rest of the class. While other students wrote things down, raised their hands and asked intelligent questions, I slumped at my desk, doodling on my otherwise blank note paper, becoming more and more frustrated, confused, and frightened. The teacher had started off by explaining that knowing how to outline was important, a skill we would need in years to come. Here I was, just not getting it. I didn't dare raise my hand to ask for help; I dreaded what I was sure the teacher would say, in front of friends and enemies: "You should have been paying better attention."

Physical education, the favorite class of many non-academically-inclined students, was among my least favorite when it involved team sports. Having a reputation for distractibility, slowness and lack of enthusiasm could make the difference between whether you were chosen first or last for a team, and after the humiliation of being among the last players chosen, you still had to play the game.

Most embarrassing of all, I cried easily, a personal failing which invited scorn and ridicule from classmates. Even some teachers reacted in dismay at the first sign of tears. In addition, my general social awkwardness (of which bursting into tears was only one example) made me wonder if other students my age belonged to a sort of Coolness Club for which I had, mysteriously, not received an invitation. Why couldn't I just grow up and act like everyone else?

School was, for me, the kind of job where you have to arrive on time and put in the required hours, with your work subject to critique at any moment, but in which the major decisions are all made by others. I couldn't hide; I couldn't blend in. Truancy laws being what they were, I couldn't even quit and get another job until they gave me permission to do so.

Eventually, as I got older, I developed better management skills and was able to cultivate a public persona that looked more like those of my peers (with the occasional embarrassing regression). Speaking of peers, I wonder now how many of them had also developed a public persona that they hoped looked like everyone else's. Had they started earlier and gotten better at it sooner? Is it possible I wasn't the only one?

The last day of school was among the happiest days of my life; I never looked back once I'd walked out of that final classroom. It was the 1970s, the era of back-to-the-land, do-it-yourself self-sufficiency, so instead of going to college, I moved with my parents and brothers to a farm homestead where I learned to care for animals, grow a garden, and preserve food. I married, raised kids, and worked at developing my art and craft skills, eventually establishing a small business selling my work. More than forty years passed.

Now here I was, preparing for re-entry into the academic world as a college student. I'd been a working artist for several decades, but I'd been giving the idea of college quite a bit of thought over the previous year or two. Ironically, I'd decided to see if this might be what would help me with the focusing issues I still had. I'd give it a good try, anyway, and if it didn't work out, well, I'd try something different, *because I could.* There were no truancy laws for people over 60. Nobody was going to send me to the principal's office or write a note to my mother. I'd taken a placement test and an interest survey, spoken with an academic advisor, applied for financial aid, signed up for my first semester, attended orientation, received a brand-new student planner and gotten a photo ID card.

I'd been chosen for the team; I still had to play the game.

At orientation, I'd been told that I had to take at least one math course. I made a quick decision and chose Probability and Statistics - my own kids had taken it, and it sounded like fun. Ha! Had I ever before chosen a math course because it *sounded* like *fun?* Had I ever chosen a math course for myself at all? I'd always simply been told what came next in the curriculum, in high school. On the other hand, was this course, in fact, too advanced for someone like me? I had scored very low on math skills in the placement test, but my advisor said I should be OK as long as I took the remedial course alongside the regular one. Together these two counted as a single course, possibly the last math course I would ever have to take - information that filled me with fervent hope.

It was the third day of class. Prob and Stats started at 8 a.m.; I had made a point of being early each day, and after the first day I wasn't even among the last people to be early. But once I was in my seat, I'd gotten absorbed in the final details of an assignment I was trying to finish for another class. I had one eye on the clock, but by the time I'd put the other assignment away and gotten out my math notebook and pencil, the professor already had her projector up and running.

Suddenly, I was lost.

I shuffled back and forth through the pages of the printed handout and scrolled down through the PowerPoint presentation on my computer monitor, but while I hunted, the professor was rapidly moving on to the next point...and the next...and the next...

Long-submerged panic came bubbling up from forty years in the past - a well-remembered inner voice.

*Just play along. Keep looking for the right place, but don't let anyone know you're lost.*

*Did you seriously think you had what it takes to succeed here?*

*It's only the third day of college. It's just going to get harder from now on.*

Frozen behind my computer monitor, frustrated and confused and a little frightened, I became aware of another inner voice, a newer, very quiet one. I fought down my panic, trying to hear what the quiet voice was telling me.

*Just ask for help. Go ahead, raise your hand. Speak up.*

*What's the worst that can happen?*

*It's only the third day of college. It's too soon to quit.*

At last, I raised my hand. "Excuse me," I blurted out, "I'm lost. Where are we?"

The professor stopped teaching and walked back to my desk. The students on either side of me leaned in to look. Together, the three of them helped me find the right page in the printed notes and scroll down to the current PowerPoint location. Then the professor said something I wasn't expecting.

"I'm sorry. I guess I was going too fast. You're probably not the only one - I bet there are other students who are just as lost as you were. Thanks for speaking up."

She went back to her projector, and I cried. Not from shame because I'd been lost or had to ask for help, but because of what she *didn't* say: "You should have been paying better attention."

The third day of college wouldn't be the last time the Prob and Stats professor had to stop the class to help me find my place, or to repeat something I just couldn't seem to understand. She continued to move fast, but she was patient with those of us who were slow to catch on, cheerful even on days when 8:00 a.m. found some of us a little sleep-deprived, always ready with clear explanations and a humorous example or two to fix in our minds a fact we would need. Her skill and patience are among the main reasons I finished that course with an A.

To my own surprise, I didn't drop out of college after the first semester. I went on to get my associate degree, then - still promising myself I could quit any time I wanted to - I took a deep breath and registered at a four-year university. Two years later, I graduated with a Bachelor of Science in Interdisciplinary Studies.

As I often tell people, I still haven't quite decided what I want to be when I grow up, and I've discovered that that's OK. I still get confused and frustrated now and then, when I lose track of what I'm supposed to be doing. Sometimes I even cry about it. But at least now I know I'm not the only one.

*Oh, and by the way, I also finally learned
the outline method of taking notes.*

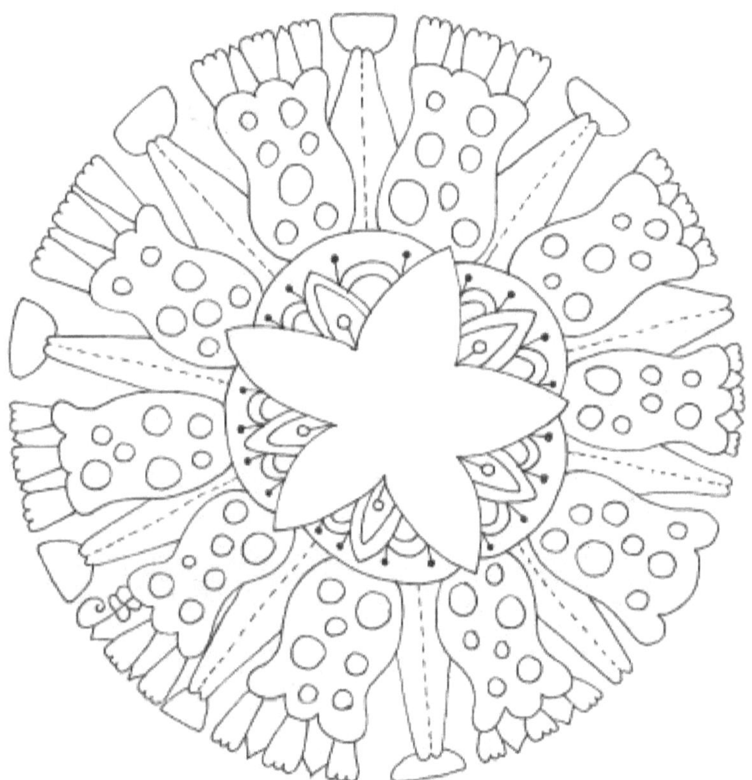

# Neat, Tidy...Creative?

If a cluttered desk is the sign of a cluttered mind,
what's an empty desk a sign of?
*Albert Einstein*

When Marie Kondo's book *The Life-Changing Magic of Tidying Up* became a bestseller, I borrowed it from the library, wondering whether I could glean anything from this popular book that would help me in my lifelong struggle with keeping things in order. Unwilling to commit as yet to her recommended marathon once-in-a-lifetime decluttering event, I nevertheless found some very good tips there.

For example, getting rid of things that don't bring joy made sense - I figured if I was going to clear out extra stuff, I might as well start with things I didn't like. So I began letting those things go. It felt good. I'm an artist and craftsperson, and every time I turned my attention to my stash of creative supplies, I realized that even here I had collected things I neither liked nor needed. So I set to work weeding them out, feeling like a superhero every time I gave away even a piece of fabric or a few skeins of yarn. Still, sometimes it was hard to know where to draw the line. *Haven't used it in a year? Five years? Ha! Try ten, or how about twenty? I regularly use something from my stash that has been there since the 1990s!*

Like Marie Kondo, I too have cast about to find a cleaning and organizing system that works for me. In some ways, however, she and I are very different. For example, at age seven she was already fascinated by the subject of household organization, even skipping recess at school to stay inside and tidy up the bookshelves in her classroom. At age seven, I was still playing with dolls, and household organization ranked so low on my list of "Interesting Ways to Spend My Time" that it probably wasn't even on the list at all.

Also unlike Ms Kondo, I never really did become fascinated by this subject. Instead, as I grew older I concentrated on things that I knew would bring me joy: my art and crafts activities. But the more my creative skills grew, the more my housekeeping skills fluctuated between mediocre and low - sometimes really, really low.

It's not that I didn't notice the mess, or that I didn't care. It's not even that I didn't try. It's not that I didn't look into existing systems (after I'd grown up) as I made an effort to bring order and beauty to my general artistic chaos. It's just that after a few weeks of trying to follow any system, I would lose interest and abandon the attempt.

I had reached senior citizenship without having mastered this skill that seemed so straightforward to so many of my friends, when I decided to temporarily set aside my chosen lifestyle as a full-time artist in favor of higher education, for the first time ever. There were several reasons why I thought this would be a good idea, but one of the main ones was that I hoped it would help me find some focus and develop discipline that would spill over into other areas of my life. Two or three years of community college, I thought, might do it - I would try for an associate degree, if I could stick it out that long. It so happened that I could, so at the end of the second year, as I made arrangements to test out of the final course

I needed for my associate degree, I pushed ahead with plans for starting work on my Bachelor's in Interdisciplinary Studies at the university where two of my children had attended.

This was the fall of 2020 coming up, and for the first time in that school's history almost everything would be online. College by remote was wonderful in many ways:

- We saved lots of money on gas, and there was no travel time to factor in.

- Nutritious and filling meals could be prepared and eaten inexpensively at home.

- Like many others, I found I could crawl out of bed five minutes before a Zoom class and still show up on time, coffee cup in hand, in T-shirt and pajama bottoms.

- The cat was allowed to attend class with me.

But being home so much also meant I was faced with my household mess *all the time.* I was annoyed with myself for not having a good, accessible place to keep my college materials, the ones I used every day, but I was so busy trying to make sure everything got done that I didn't want to take the time to clear a spot. I was surrounded by clutter that got in the way, tipped over, spilled onto things, obscured the books and files I actually needed, and frustrated me by its persistence. In addition, the COVID-19 pandemic was ongoing, with its associated anxieties and limitations and its devastating effects on thousands of people, including friends and family members. That third year of college, the first year of the pandemic, the year on remote, I finally reached out for help.

McKenzie, the counselor I was referred to by Student Services, was the same age as my middle daughter, but she was patient as well as knowledgeable about college students. We talked about the trouble I was having keeping up with my increased course load during this third year, and, eventually, I began to share about my struggles with getting the house cleaned and decluttered - struggles which had only gotten worse since I started college. "And when I do have a little time, I rush to do something creative instead of buckling down to get things tidied up the way they should be," I told her.

McKenzie listened. Then she gave me a link to an exercise[5] in which I would go through a list of personal values and pick out the ten I felt were most important to me. After that, I was to go through my top ten again and pick out my top five. Finally, I was to pick out my top two. When I had done this and returned the next week with my top-two values, she suggested that keeping those two values in mind could help me find a way to get my housekeeping done.

"As I've listened to you tell your story," she explained, "it sounds to me as if you really don't like having other people tell you what to do. So just following a system designed by someone else isn't going to work. You need to associate your housekeeping tasks with what you yourself feel is most important - your 'top-two' values. Then you can use what motivates you the most, rather than fighting against yourself. But you need to make room for your creative activities, too, alongside the cleaning and organizing you want to get done, because that's what brings you joy."

Working with my own values rather than trying to force myself to conform to what motivated someone else was a new thought for me. Before the end of the semester in May, I had begun planning my upcoming summer around several key goals. One of them was the decluttering project I had been thinking about for months, but I also included plans for spending time in the clay studio at the local Senior Center to catch up on as many of my requests for pottery as possible, in preparation for the coming winter when the pressure of schoolwork might mean I would not have time to make things. There was some sewing I needed to do for the family, and I wanted to reserve time for exercise, building it into my more flexible summer routine. Then, as the weeks passed and I began putting my plans into action (enlisting my husband's help for some of the bigger projects) I started doing some writing, too, when it turned out that a quiet writing session was a natural follow-up activity to exercise time.

The fall semester of my senior year in college was just a couple of weeks away when I stopped, looked around, and realized that while the house wasn't perfect yet, it was in better working order than it had been at the beginning of the summer. We'd cleared a few cupboards and countertops (some for the first time in years) and thrown away a lot of stuff. One project I was particularly pleased about was the redesigning and rebuilding of our clumsy "afterthought" kitchen pantry using shelving we already had on hand, so we could now easily see and reach everything inside. I'd finished a lot of pottery and was on my way to finishing the sewing projects I'd started, I'd made quite a bit of progress knitting a gift for a family member, I'd completed a long-overdue portrait request and a sketchbook of meditative drawings, and I'd written at least ten stories. Sometimes I even got enough sleep! No, I hadn't undertaken the marathon "tidying up" Marie Kondo explains so well in her first book, but I had succeeded in getting something significant done during the summer - several things, in fact, on which I could look back, see change, and appreciate progress.

Has my time in college led to more discipline in the rest of my life? I graduated in the spring of 2022; I'm organizing my life differently after having the experience (often stressful) of juggling more responsibilities than I cared to over the previous four years as a college student. Perhaps one day I'll initiate a KonMari tidying marathon and get rid of the worst of the clutter for good. Meanwhile, it's unlikely any method I might invent and write a book about will be in competition with *The Life-Changing Magic of Tidying Up*. Each person, after all, has her own gift to give the world. But at least by then I'll probably have cleared a good place to keep my research materials.

[1] www.ravelry.com/patterns/library/pomatomus

[2] "7 Health Reasons to Take Up Knitting." US News and World Report, Nov. 17, 2016.

[3] "Pocket Fairy," design by Gingermelon on Etsy.

[4] Decades later, I found the missing sleeve. It was shared by another dress pattern on a different page.

[5] www.think2perform.com/values/

# Don't miss out!

Visit the website below and you can sign up to receive emails whenever Barbara Bell publishes a new book. There's no charge and no obligation.

https://books2read.com/r/B-A-PQDGB-VTNAD

**BOOKS 2 READ**

Connecting independent readers to independent writers.

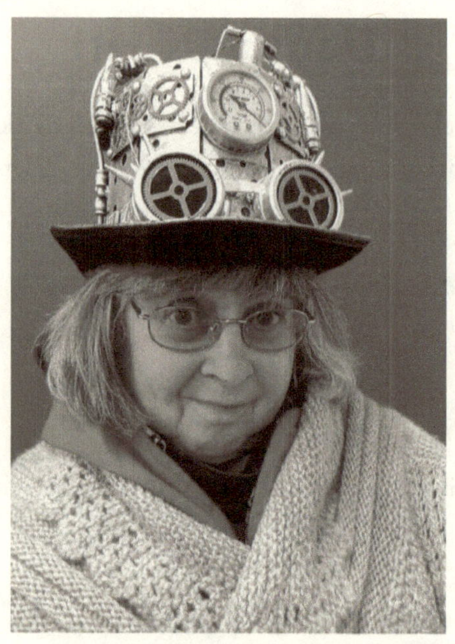

# About the Author

Barbara Bell has been making art and crafts since she was able to hold a crayon without eating it. Surrounded by creative family and friends, teachers, mentors, books, and plenty of opportunities for practice and daydreaming, she divides her time unequally in many directions. She and her husband Peter have lived in Canada and Japan but now reside in upper east Tennessee.

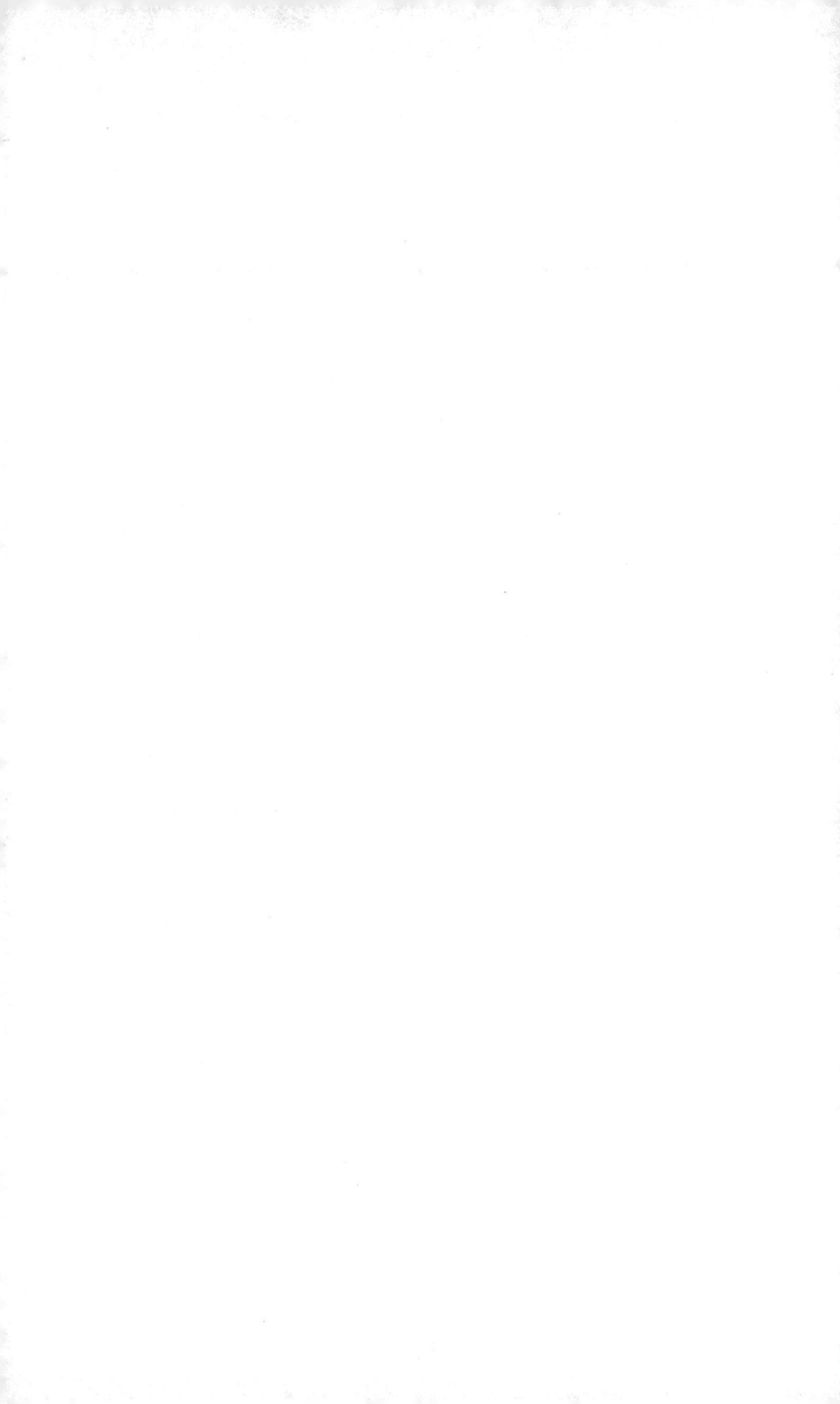